P9-DFP-142

WILLIAM LLOYD GARRISON

ABOLITIONIST AND JOURNALIST

SPECIAL LIVES IN HISTORY THAT BECOME

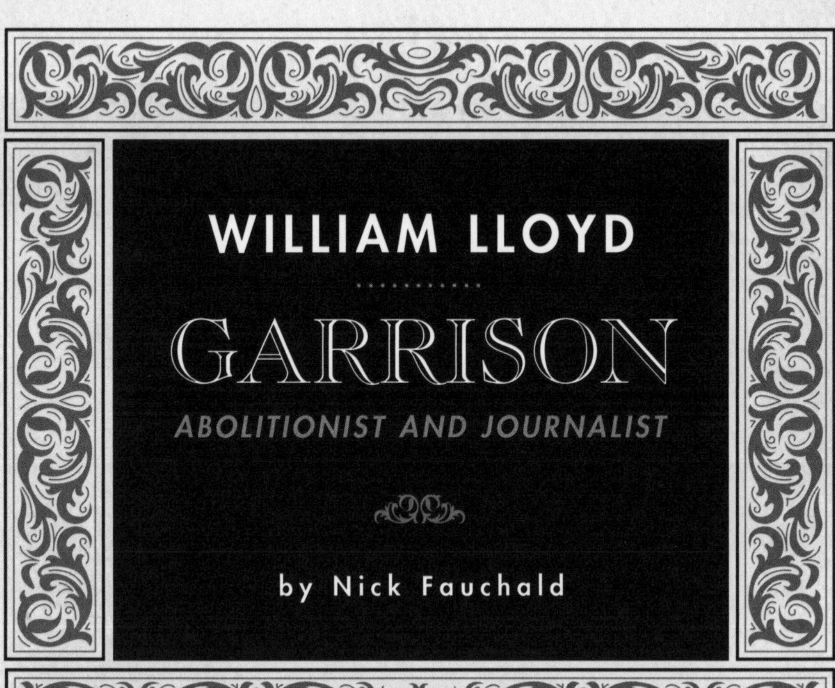

WILLIAM LLOYD GARRISON

ABOLITIONIST AND JOURNALIST

by Nick Fauchald

Content Adviser: Lisa Laskin, Ph.D.,
Lecturer on History,
Harvard University

Reading Adviser: Rosemary G. Palmer, Ph.D.,
Department of Literacy, College of Education
Boise State University

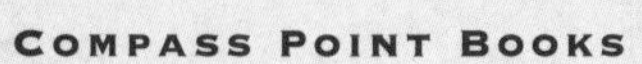
COMPASS POINT BOOKS  MINNEAPOLIS, MINNESOTA

Compass Point Books
3109 West 50th Street, #115
Minneapolis, MN 55410

Visit Compass Point Books on the Internet at *www.compasspointbooks.com*
or e-mail your request to *custserv@compasspointbooks.com*

Editor: Jill Kalz
Lead Designer: Jaime Martens
Photo Researcher: Marcie C. Spence
Page Production: Heather Griffin, Bobbie Nuytten
Cartographer: XNR Productions, Inc.
Educational Consultant: Diane Smolinski

Managing Editor: Catherine Neitge
Art Director: Keith Griffin
Production Director: Keith McCormick
Creative Director: Terri Foley

Library of Congress Cataloging-in-Publication Data
Fauchald, Nick.
William Lloyd Garrison : abolitionist and journalist / by Nick Fauchald.
p. cm. — (Signature lives)
Includes bibliographical references and index.
ISBN 0-7565-0819-3 (hardcover)
1. Garrison, William Lloyd, 1805–1879—Juvenile literature. 2. Abolitionists—United States—Biography—Juvenile literature. 3. Antislavery movements—United States—History—19th century—Juvenile literature. I. Title. II. Series.
E449.G25F38 2005
973.7'114'092—dc22 2004019870

Printed in the United States of America.

Signature Lives

CIVIL WAR ERA

The Civil War (1861–1865) split the United States into two countries and divided the people over the issue of slavery. The opposing sides—the Union in the North and the Confederacy in the South—battled each other for four long years in the deadliest American conflict ever fought. The bloody war sometimes pitted family members and friends against each other over the issues of slavery and states' rights. Some of the people who lived and served their country during the Civil War are among the nation's most beloved heroes.

William Lloyd Garrison

Table of Contents

Chapter 1

Discovering the Press

Lloyd didn't want to make cabinets. He was 11 years old, miles from his family, and feeling homesick. He was small for his age, too, and not very strong. Cabinetmaking in 1817 was physically demanding work, and Lloyd wasn't naturally good at it. Perhaps most important, he didn't see how building furniture would help him make a difference in the world. But his mother had found him the apprenticeship, and he had promised her that, unlike his older brother, who had run away from their home in Massachusetts to live a life at sea, he would find honest work and grow up to be a respectable man. Lloyd was now bound by a contract to serve his master, Moses Short, for seven years. To the boy, it seemed like a lifetime. And he really didn't want to make cabinets.

As an adult, William Lloyd Garrison looked like a mild-mannered school teacher, but he was a fiery preacher on the subject of abolishing slavery.

Despite their name, cabinetmakers make more than cabinets. These highly skilled woodworkers also create such items as dining tables, bookcases, clock cases, and chests of drawers. In the early 19th century, cabinetmakers decorated furniture surfaces with exotic wood inlays and very thin layers of wood called veneers.

One morning, when his master was out of the shop, Lloyd decided to leave. He jumped out the back window, ran to where the stagecoach stopped, and leapt on board. But once Short discovered his apprentice was missing, he hitched up his wagon and caught up to the young runaway. Lloyd explained how much he disliked his new trade and begged Short to allow him to return home. Short, who was a kind man, finally agreed, and in doing so cleared the way for Lloyd to discover his true calling, the career path he was meant to follow: publishing.

A few years later, in 1819, just before Lloyd's 14th birthday, Ephriam W. Allen, who owned and edited a local newspaper, the *Newburyport Herald*, offered the boy a seven-year apprenticeship.

Lloyd saw that the publishing business could get a man noticed. He was excited about his new trade and first learned how to set type—to line up little metal letters in a box to form words, sentences, and paragraphs. Years later, he remembered his first days at the *Newburyport Herald:*

Printers, shoemakers, blacksmiths and other tradespeople learned their craft through apprenticeships.

I never shall forget the surprise and amazement which I felt on first being led to the case to see the types set and distributed with such celerity by those who were familiar with the work, and my little heart sank like lead within me. It seemed to me that I never should be able to do anything of the kind. However, I was put to learn the different boxes and to ascertain where the capitals and small capitals were placed and, in the lower case, how the types were diversified, and very soon learned the whole. Then I took the composing stick and began to set types, and from that day to this I have delighted in nothing more, as regards manual work, than the manipulation of types.

Garrison's greatest contribution to the antislavery movement was his newspaper, The Liberator.

Even though Lloyd was so small that he needed to stand on a large weight in order to reach the typesetting box, he quickly became very fast and accurate at his work. Allen was impressed and promoted his apprentice to office foreman, making him responsible for preparing the entire newspaper for printing.

Lloyd was pleased with this new career: It brought public recognition; it wasn't too physically demanding; and it would give him the opportunity to influence many people. Throughout his life, he said it was destiny that found him the apprenticeship with Allen. And the boy known as William Lloyd Garrison would soon discover another benefit of working at a newspaper: He could voice his own opinions, ones that would eventually make him famous as a leader of the antislavery movement.

William Lloyd Garrison was one of the most important figures in the fight to end slavery in the

United States, and perhaps the most controversial. For more than three decades—from his days as a young abolitionist in the 1830s until the end of the Civil War—Garrison insisted that the millions of slaves in the United States be freed. Many others were also attempting to abolish slavery, but Garrison stood out from his peers because he was determined to free all slaves immediately, and without exception. Garrison refused to rest until he achieved this goal, and his unwavering stubbornness kept him unsettled for most of his life.

Garrison was one of the most hated men of his time. Even his supporters thought his ideas were too extreme, and his fiercest enemies cried for his blood. He was dragged through the streets of Boston, Massachusetts, thrown into jail, almost lynched and threatened at every turn, but Garrison never backed down from his demand for an immediate end to slavery until his prophecy was fulfilled.

"I WILL BE HEARD." Garrison wrote this declaration in the first issue of his famous abolitionist newspaper, *The Liberator.* And he was heard, and still is, even today.

Chapter 2 The Early Years

On December 12, 1805, in the busy port town of Newburyport, Massachusetts, Abijah and Fanny Garrison became parents for the third time. Four-year-old James and 2-year-old Caroline had a new baby brother, William Lloyd, whom their mother called Lloyd.

Lloyd's father was a sea captain and had recently moved his family to Newburyport from Canada to find more work. He sailed ships up and down the East Coast and transported goods to faraway places such as the West Indies. Newburyport's shipping industry was bustling at that time, and for a couple of years Abijah had no trouble providing for his family.

But in 1807, when Lloyd was 2 years old, hard times fell on the Garrison family. The U.S. Congress

As a young man, Garrison considered becoming a preacher to spread his ideas about how to rid the world of evils such as slavery and alcohol.

passed the Embargo Act, which stopped trade with foreign countries. President Thomas Jefferson declared that all American trading ships must remain at their docks. Local trade along the coast wasn't enough to make a living, and empty ships stayed tied up in Newburyport's once-busy harbor.

Abijah couldn't find work. Instead, he spent his time in the town's pubs, drinking with the other unemployed seamen. Fanny, a devout Christian, disapproved of this behavior and often told Abijah and his friends that their drinking was evil in the eyes of God. But Abijah didn't listen. One night, he brought home a bottle of rum and some of his drunken friends, and Fanny chased them out, smashing the bottle in front of them.

William Lloyd Garrison's hometown of Newburyport, Massachusetts, is located on the south bank of the Merrimack River at the mouth of the Atlantic Ocean. Originally inhabited by the Pawtucket Indians, the area was later settled by European immigrants who founded the city of Newbury in the 1630s. By 1764, the port was so prosperous that it broke off from Newbury to form Newburyport. Today, the city is home to more than 17,000 inhabitants.

A tragedy hit the family a year later, when 5-year-old Caroline ate some poisonous flower petals that had been thrown out by one of the Garrisons' neighbors. Caroline died, and the family was grief-stricken. Two months later, Fanny gave birth to a baby girl, Maria Elizabeth, but she and

The Garrison family lived in a few rooms of this house in Newburyport, Massachusetts.

Abijah continued to grieve for Caroline. Still unable to find work, Abijah continued to drink heavily, and in July 1808 he left his family and never returned. Fanny was now alone with three small children to raise by herself.

Without a husband and a regular source of income, Fanny went to work for the town's wealthy families, caring for their sick, emptying their kitchen and bathroom waste, and washing their linens. She left her children with a neighbor, Martha Farnham, while she worked. When times were particularly hard, and the family was short of food, she sometimes had Lloyd sell molasses candy on the street or sent him with a tin pan to her employers' homes to beg for leftovers. This last task was the most humiliating for Lloyd, especially when other young boys would stop him and demand to know what was in

Garrison spent much of his life in the northeastern United States.

the pan. Someday, he promised himself, he would fight back against the kind of bullies who teased him for collecting scraps of food.

Fanny was very religious and raised Lloyd, John, and Maria to be the same, giving them lessons from the Bible and teaching them strict moral beliefs. When he could, Lloyd attended school, but much of the time he needed to work to earn money to support his family. He was a smart boy, but learning to read and write was difficult for him. To make matters worse, his schoolteacher insisted he write with his right hand, even though he was naturally left-handed.

By 1812, most of Newburyport's population had moved to other towns due to the failing shipping industry. Fanny had trouble finding work. She moved to Lynn, Massachusetts, taking her older son, James, with her. Lynn was a center for the shoemaking trade, so she hoped to find him work as a shoemaker's apprentice. Fanny left Maria and Lloyd in Newburyport with friends. Maria went to live with a neighbor, and Lloyd roomed with Ezekial Bartlett and his family. Ezekial was a poor woodcutter and leader of the Baptist church the Garrisons attended. The Bartletts continued to teach Lloyd Christian values, but they kept him too busy with household chores to attend much school.

Lloyd worked hard to write with his right hand.

In the early 1800s, when Garrison was a boy, one-room schoolhouses were common.

He stayed in at recess to practice until he could write his name perfectly. His handwriting soon became so neat that his teacher had it displayed in the window of the Newburyport bank.

Lloyd's brother became a shoemaker's apprentice in Lynn, but by the time he was 14 years old,

James was already mirroring his father's behavior by drinking heavily, getting into fights, and arguing with his mother when she scolded him.

Shoemakers began opening shops all across Massachusetts during the late 1700s, and by the time William Lloyd Garrison was a boy, shoemaking was one of the most important industries in the state. Masters passed on their knowledge to apprentices. The towns of Lynn, Brocton, and Haverhill were key shoemaking centers.

In 1815, Fanny sent for Lloyd, and she and her sons moved to Baltimore, Maryland, where she found them shoemaker apprenticeships at a new factory. Lloyd, now 9 years old, was small and weak for his age and had trouble keeping up with the hard work of making shoes. The long days of hammering and sewing left his hands and arms bruised and sore. Luckily for him, the factory closed soon after it opened. But his brother also lost his apprenticeship, which fueled James's drinking problem. Like his father, James wanted to be a sea captain. The shipping trade was coming alive again in Baltimore, and sea captains were hiring crews. James decided to do what his father had done years before: he ran away to be a sailor.

Losing another family member to a life at sea devastated Fanny, but she was determined to stay in Baltimore, where work was easier to find than in Newburyport. Lloyd, however, was very unhappy

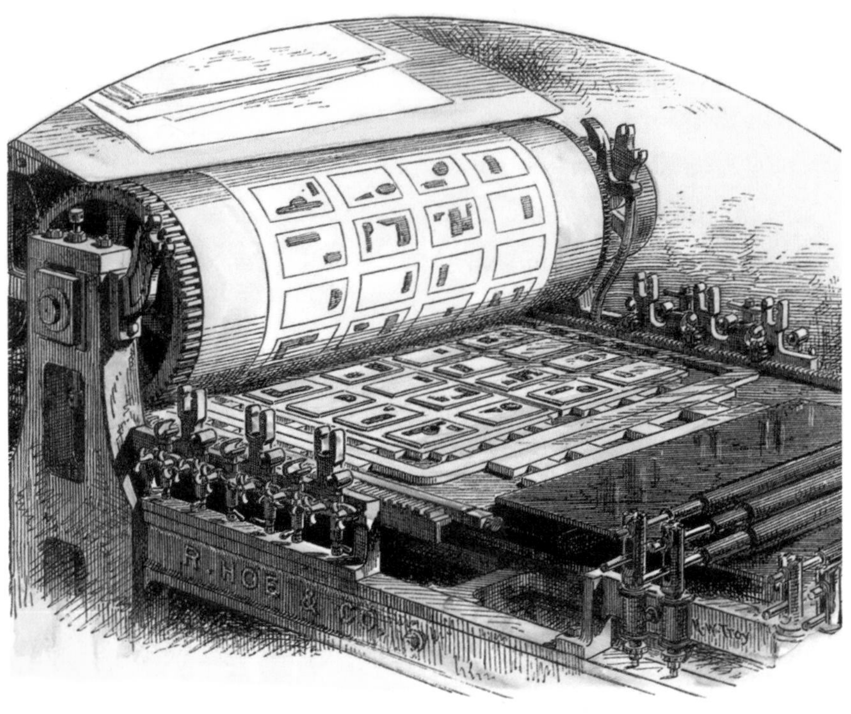

The printing press would become Garrison's tool for spreading his antislavery message.

living in Baltimore. He was ashamed of his brother's behavior and his family's poverty. When he was 10 years old, he finally convinced his mother to let him return to Newburyport on his own.

In the fall of 1816, Lloyd moved back in with the Bartlett family. On Sundays, he sang in the church choir. He had a big voice for such a small boy and would write his mother and tell her about how he enjoyed singing. Lloyd always wanted to make his mother proud of him.

The following year, Fanny again sent for Lloyd. She had found him a woodworking apprenticeship in a town called Haverhill, Massachusetts. As an apprentice, Lloyd would have to work seven years, learning to build cabinets from a man named Moses Short. Lloyd went to live in the Shorts' home, but he hated his new job. He ran away, but his master soon caught up with him. After listening to Lloyd's pleas, Short released him from his contract.

In 1819, Ephriam W. Allen, owner of the *Newburyport Herald*, agreed to take Lloyd on as his apprentice for the next seven years, and so began Lloyd's career as a newspaperman.

Chapter 3 Young Writer and Editor

When he was 16, Lloyd wrote his first newspaper article. He had been setting type for other people's words—why not his own? He thought he was still too young to be taken seriously, so he wrote his first story anonymously. He had heard about a young man in Boston, Massachusetts, who had dated a woman for two years and then refused to marry her—not an acceptable behavior in the 1820s. A judge fined the man $750 for breaking his promise. Lloyd was angry that a woman should have so much power over a man. So he sat down and wrote a letter to the *Herald* explaining his disagreement about the fine imposed for the incident. He disguised his perfect handwriting and signed the letter "An Old Bachelor," ending his piece with the following: "For

Like the apprentice pictured here, Garrison learned to assemble pages of text by picking individual metal letters from boxes by hand and laying them out to form words.

my part, notwithstanding, I am determined to lead the single life and not trouble myself about the ladies."

Lloyd feared that his employer would recognize him as the author of the letter when he entered the print shop the next day and perhaps reprimand him for his actions. Allen, however, was smiling. He enjoyed the letter so much that he read it aloud to the *Herald* staff and had Lloyd set it in type for printing. He had no idea Lloyd had written it.

Pleased with the printing of his first piece of writing, Lloyd was anxious to write more. Each week, he wrote another letter, signing it with the initials "A.O.B.," and slipped it under the post office door. Allen grew fond of "An Old Bachelor," not knowing it was his own apprentice, and encouraged more writing from the unnamed writer. He even placed an ad in the *Herald* asking the anonymous author if he would consider writing regularly for the newspaper. And he wanted to meet "A.O.B." in person.

Lloyd was terrified. If he confessed his identity, would Allen fire him? He decided to take the chance. Surprisingly, Allen was pleased with his apprentice's courage and asked him to write more frequently.

Lloyd wrote his mother to tell her of his accomplishments. She wrote back, telling him that she had mixed feelings about his new profession. Writers, she warned, often starved to death long

By 1850, advanced presses such as this one were enabling printers to do in a couple hours what once took an entire day.

before anyone learned to appreciate them. She thought Lloyd's time would be better spent reading the Bible, believing heavenly rewards were greater than those on Earth. But she didn't want to turn away another son, and gave in. "But as it is done," she wrote, "I suppose you think you had better go on

By 1825, Baltimore, Maryland, was a prosperous milling city, with more than 60 flour mills located near the city center.

and seek the Applause of Mortals."

By the spring of 1823, Lloyd had not seen his mother for seven years. She wrote him often, urging him to visit her in Baltimore. She had fallen ill and knew it wouldn't be long until her sickness would take her life. Allen, an understanding man, gave 18-year-old Lloyd enough time off to go visit his mother.

When mother and son were finally reunited, Fanny broke down into tears, and Lloyd hardly recognized her in her weakened condition. She appeared quite pale and thin. He wrote Allen:

> *You must imagine my sensations on beholding a dearly beloved mother, after an absence of seven years. I found her in tears—but O God, so altered, so emaciated, that I should never have recognized her.*

Fanny Garrison died two months after her son's visit, but Lloyd would feel her influence for his entire life. He credited her for giving him her best qualities: determination, independence, stubbornness, and the courage to speak out against those who failed to meet his strict moral standards. But Lloyd was alone now, without a family (his sister Maria had fallen ill and died in 1822), and that pain burned inside him.

Lloyd continued writing during the final two years of his apprenticeship at the *Herald.* Instead of voicing his opinions about human interest stories as "An Old Bachelor," he shifted to the subject of politics. He read other newspapers and copied the style of writers he admired. Although he was still too young to vote, he had no trouble telling the people of Newburyport whom to support in the upcoming presidential election.

In the presidential election of 1824, Lloyd wrote articles against both leading candidates, John Quincy Adams and Andrew Jackson. Instead, he supported William Crawford, a politician from Georgia whom Lloyd thought was the most moral of the candidates. Adams won, and Crawford finished next to last, but Lloyd had established himself as a political writer. He had much to say on many subjects and enjoyed the influence he had on people.

In the 19th century, newspapers were the most powerful tools in politics. Editors wrote very favorably about those politicians they supported, and they attacked those they opposed. During the 1824 U.S. presidential election, various newspapers made fun of John Quincy Adams's wife and clothes; they charged that candidate William Crawford had committed unlawful acts while in office; and some even accused General Andrew Jackson of murder.

Lloyd was unsure where destiny would take him. He wanted his voice to be heard by people everywhere, but working at a small town newspaper wouldn't make him famous. Even though his mother had passed away, he also wanted to make her proud and hoped he could spread the Christian word, promoting good morals and striking down sin wherever it occurred. He considered becoming a preacher, but he felt he wasn't educated enough, and very few preachers extended their influence beyond their town's borders. He *could* get a free education if he joined the military, but he thought about his mother and how she had hated violence. Writing and editing, spreading his messages through the written word, would be his path to success.

At the conclusion of Lloyd's apprenticeship in 1826, Allen helped him purchase his own newspaper, which he named *The Free Press.* Now Lloyd was his own boss and could freely publish his own opinions. He believed that politics should conform above all to Christian values, and he didn't mind telling his readers so. Lloyd was loyal to the old Federalist Party, a conservative political group that favored a strong, centralized government. The party was declining steadily in popularity, but Lloyd still wrote articles promoting Federalist views, even though many of his subscribers supported other political parties.

Before his unsuccessful run for the U.S. presidency in 1824, William Crawford practiced law and served as a senator from the state of Georgia.

But Lloyd was stubborn and refused to tone down his opinions. He even insulted the man who had given him his start in publishing. Lloyd wrote an article criticizing the *Herald,* Allen's newspaper, for praising the accomplishments of Thomas Jefferson

Garrison's participation in church activities as a child in Newburyport laid the groundwork for the deep religious faith he possessed as an adult.

upon his death on July 4, 1826. Lloyd called Allen a hypocrite for writing in favor of someone who didn't hold strong religious beliefs.

People cancelled their subscriptions to *The Free*

Press, and Lloyd was forced to sell his paper. Newburyport was too small a town for his radical ideas, so he left for Boston in late 1826. In Boston, Lloyd believed he could influence more people and help them recognize the evils that he believed were strangling politics and society. He had a lot of ideas in his head, important ideas, and they needed to be heard. It wouldn't be easy to convince people to listen and change their ways, but Lloyd was more than ready to try. The once-poor boy who had shamefully begged for food scraps with a tin plate had matured into a man who would stand up for his beliefs, no matter what obstacles he faced.

Boston, Massachusetts, was the site of such Revolutionary War events as the Boston Tea Party and the Boston Massacre. It was from Boston that Paul Revere made his famous ride to warn people that the British soldiers were coming. In the mid-1900s, Boston became a center for finance and learning, boasting such universities as Harvard, MIT, and others.

Chapter 4 Birth of an Abolitionist

At first, life in Boston in 1826 was difficult for William Lloyd Garrison. After investing all of his money into a newspaper that had failed, he was penniless and couldn't find steady work. For almost a year he wandered the streets of Boston in worn-out shoes and tattered clothes, hungry, finding only temporary jobs that offered little pay.

Garrison finally got his break the following summer when he was hired as the editor of Boston's *National Philanthropist*, a newspaper that appreciated Garrison's beliefs. The *Philanthropist* supported temperance, the idea that alcohol—which had poisoned the lives of Garrison's father and brother—was bad and should be avoided by everyone. At his new job, Garrison spoke out against alcohol and other

In the early 1800s, Garrison met many people who were willing to listen to his antislavery message in Boston, Massachusetts.

vices, such as gambling, swearing, and dancing. He also spoke out against war and in favor of peaceful resolution. And more and more, he wrote about slavery and the nation's poor. From his own childhood experiences, he understood the pain and hardship of being poor and sympathized with the slaves' struggle against oppression.

Abolitionists traveled from town to town spreading their antislavery message to anyone who would listen.

And while most of the *Philanthropist's* readers agreed that slavery was wrong, they felt it wasn't their concern. Slavery was the South's problem, they thought, and they objected to the new editor's

radical messages. Many people stopped buying the paper. Because of the loss of readership, Garrison lost his job within six months.

But by the time he left the *Philanthropist* in 1828, Garrison had made connections with many others who believed that sin was the source of the nation's problems, and that the only way to fix these problems was to avoid sinful behavior and practice temperance. Garrison felt it was God's will that had given him his role as social reformer, and it was his responsibility to carry out this duty. His future as an abolitionist was built upon this belief.

Another influence on Garrison's abolitionist career was Benjamin Lundy. Lundy was one of America's most important opponents of slavery. Like Garrison, Lundy was a thin, frail New Englander. When he was 19, Lundy visited a slave market in Virginia and saw slaves for the first time. His life was forever changed. He saw slaves being chained and dragged aboard ships bound for southern plantations. He heard the cries of little children being separated from their mothers. Soon after this encounter, Lundy began walking from state to state starting local antislavery societies. He had been attacked and almost killed by slave owners. By the time he met Garrison, Lundy had visited 19 states and walked thousands of miles. He had started his own newspaper, called the *Genius of Universal*

Emancipation, but with his busy schedule and little writing experience he had trouble getting it printed on a regular basis.

Garrison was impressed with Lundy's cause. Lundy helped him realize that owning slaves represented the worst of the immorality that Garrison had criticized in his former newspapers. Garrison agreed to help revive Lundy's newspaper.

The key to saving the country, Garrison believed, was immediately freeing all slaves. This belief would bring Garrison many enemies and public disapproval, even threats against his life, but he had found a cause that he could stand behind with passion and conviction. Garrison was anxious to begin publishing the new *Genius* right away, but Lundy wanted more time to gather additional support. The two agreed to meet again in a few months to discuss details of the publication.

Benjamin Lundy was born in Sussex County, New Jersey. He was an editor and a pioneer of the antislavery movement in the United States. In 1815, Lundy organized the Abolitionist Union Humane Society in St. Clairsville, Ohio. He later organized other antislavery groups and published The Genius of Universal Emancipation, *the* National Enquirer, *and other periodicals. Lundy lectured and traveled widely on his crusade for the emancipation of slaves.*

Meanwhile, Garrison took a new job in Bennington, Vermont, as the editor of the *Journal of the Times*. He was hired to write favorably about U.S. President John Quincy Adams, who in 1829 was running for reelection against Andrew Jackson, a supporter of slavery. But Garrison was most interested in expressing his opinions about slavery. He wrote many stories about slaves being sold in Washington, D.C., and urged support of legislation that would ban slavery in the nation's capital. But Garrison wrote very little in support of President Adams, which made his employers unhappy with their new editor.

Benjamin Lundy was an inspiration to Garrison for his devotion to the antislavery movement.

Garrison left this position and returned to Boston, seeking a printing job that would support him until his meeting with Lundy. The Boston Congregational Society was impressed with Garrison's work and invited him to speak at a Fourth of July gathering at the Park Street Church in Boston in 1829. Although nervous about delivering his first public speech, Garrison accepted the chance to speak out against slavery:

Slaves were sold like cattle to the highest bidder, with family members often being split between buyers.

Every Fourth of July, our Declaration of Independence is produced with a sublime indignation, to set forth the tyranny of the mother country … But what a pitiful detail of the grievances does this document present, in comparison with the wrongs which our slaves endure! … I am ashamed of my country. I am sick of … our hypocritical cant about the unalienable rights of man."

The United States, Garrison said, was two-faced, meaning it was quick to acknowledge that it had been wronged by Great Britain, that the American people were entitled to their freedom, but it was refusing to acknowledge the oppression of slaves within its own borders. The 1776 Declaration of Independence stated that "all men are created equal," but blacks were clearly not being treated the same as whites. Garrison finished his speech to wild applause. His first of many public speeches was a success.

He then moved to Baltimore, where he and Lundy made preparations for the new *Genius*. But there was a problem. Even though they agreed that slavery was wrong and should be eliminated, they had different solutions to the problem. Lundy believed, as did many others who opposed slavery, that slaves should gradually be freed. What would happen to slave owners who suddenly lost their sources of labor? Who would pay for the slaves' freedom?

Garrison wouldn't stand for it. Those questions weren't important to him. Immediate emancipation, he said, was the only solution. All slaves, everywhere, should be freed right away. This kind of thinking, Lundy feared, would turn away future supporters of their cause. Garrison didn't care. In the end, the partners reached an agreement: They would write their articles separately, each signing his name to his own work. On September 8, 1829, the first edition of the *Genius* was published. Garrison didn't hesitate to express his opinions. He wrote, "As a very large proportion of our colored people were born on American soil, they are at liberty to choose their own dwelling place, and we possess no right to use coercive [forceful] measure in their removal."

Garrison's article caused a stir in Baltimore. Even members of the antislavery societies didn't completely agree with Garrison's controversial ideas. Garrison didn't believe that an entire race should be forced into submission just because of the color of their skin. What if the slaves were white? Then, he supposed, people would think otherwise.

> *I have often thought that, should God see fit, by a miracle, to change their color, straighten their hair and give their features and complexion the appearance of whites, slavery would not continue a year … But is it a suitable cause for making men slaves, because God has given them such a color, such hair and such features as he saw fit.*

Those who supported slavery—and there were many in Maryland in the late 1820s—were even more vocal in their opposition to Garrison's calls for "universal emancipation." Newspapers criticized him for being unpatriotic. But Garrison didn't mind the criticism. In fact, he gladly welcomed it. Any publicity was good publicity, he thought, even if it

attacked him personally. And one of the most famous attacks against Garrison's ideas would arrive sooner than he expected.

Slaves were often moved from place to place in chained groups called coffles.

Chapter 5 I Will Be Heard

In the spring of 1829, Garrison added a section to the newspaper that he called the "Black List." This list provided detailed accounts of the slave trade in Baltimore. Garrison learned of a ship named the *Francis*, which had recently left Baltimore for New Orleans, Louisiana, carrying 75 slaves who were chained below deck. Francis Todd, a man from Garrison's own hometown of Newburyport, owned the boat. Worse yet, Todd lived in one of the grand houses on High Street, where Garrison's mother had cared for the wealthy citizens, and Garrison had begged for food with his tin plate.

Garrison was outraged and quickly wrote about his findings in the *Genius*. He called Todd and the ship's captain, Nicholas Brown, "highway robbers

Garrison believed strongly in his mission as a social reformer, and the more opposition he faced, the harder he fought.

and murderers" and called for them to be "sentenced to solitary confinement for life" for their involvement in the slave trade.

This public declaration, as Garrison had anticipated, reached an enraged Todd, who immediately hired a lawyer. Todd didn't consider himself a robber or a murderer and filed a lawsuit against Garrison and Lundy seeking $5,000 in damages. It was illegal to make false accusations in print. On April 30, 1830, a jury found Garrison guilty of libel and sentenced him to pay $100 or spend six months in jail. Garrison didn't have the money to pay the fine, nor would he ask any of his friends for a loan. Imprisonment would only bring more attention to his cause, so four days later, Garrison happily entered the Baltimore city jail to begin serving his sentence.

An estimated 15 million Africans were transported by ship to the Americas between 1540 and 1850. Even though the United States officially got out of the international slave trade in 1808, many slaves were brought in illegally after that date. Slaves were chained together by their hands and feet and had little room to move. A large number died on the journey from diseases that spread quickly in the horribly unsanitary conditions. Many slaves were crippled for life as a consequence of the way they were confined on the ships.

Garrison saw his time behind bars as an opportunity to write more for the cause of abolishing slavery. On his first morning in jail he wrote an antislavery poem on

Newly bought slaves were shipped to their owners' estates carrying little more than the clothes on their backs.

the wall of his cell. He sent out many letters about his case, some to friends, others to editors of other newspapers. One letter began:

> *Now don't look amazed because I am in confinement. I have neither broken any man's head nor picked any man's pocket ... Yet true it is, I am in prison, as a robin in his cage. But I sing as often, and quite as well, as before my wings were clipped.*

The letters received by the editors caused many to write about Garrison's confinement. Many were sympathetic to the young abolitionist. One editor agreed with Garrison that his only so-called crime was exposing the true horrors of slavery.

Garrison's name was known across the country in a matter of weeks. Abolitionists in other cities invited him to speak in front of their antislavery societies. A very wealthy New York merchant named Arthur Tappan sent Garrison $200: half to pay for his release and the other half to keep the struggling *Genius* afloat. Garrison was a free man, more important a famous one, and his head was full of ideas.

Arthur Tappan helped fund the Underground Railroad, a secret system that helped thousands of runaway slaves escape to the North or Canada.

He wanted to start an antislavery newspaper in Washington, D.C., but had no luck raising money in a city that still allowed slaves to be traded on its streets. So he traveled to New York, to thank Tappan for his support. He traveled to Philadelphia, Pennsylvania, and New Haven, Connecticut, to speak in front of antislavery groups and meet former slaves. He visited churches attended by freed slaves and gave them his sympathy. In return, they offered him food and a place to sleep.

Meanwhile, the *Genius* could no longer support itself. Although they agreed on the same basic goal—to free the slaves—Garrison and Lundy decided to part ways. Their approaches toward reaching that goal were simply too different.

Garrison moved back to Boston to start his next newspaper. It would be a newspaper unlike any that he had published before. It would expose the evils of society and the slave trade, promote a life of good morals, and, most important, it would be all his own. But first, the penniless Garrison had to gain supporters and find enough money to print his publication.

Arthur Tappan was born in Northampton, Massachusetts, on May 22, 1786. He acquired his wealth through business investments and a silk-importing firm. Tappan held strict moral beliefs and contributed greatly to the fight against alcohol and tobacco use. He also helped fund several antislavery journals and in 1831 helped establish the United States' first Anti-Slavery Society in New York. Two years later, when the Society became a national organization, Tappan was elected its first president.

Garrison walked around Boston to find a location where he could hold meetings to gather supporters for his new venture. He didn't have enough money to rent a hall, so he asked various churches to lend him the use of their facilities. None would do so. He even put an ad in the *Boston Courier* asking for a place in

Antislavery society meetings gave their members a chance to openly share ideas and opinions.

which "to vindicate [secure] the rights of TWO MILLIONS of American citizens who are now groaning in servile chains in this boasted land of liberty; and also to propose measures for their relief."

The First Society of Free Enquirers answered his ad and offered their space. Garrison had his location. After the first meeting, two abolitionist ministers approached Garrison with an offer. Reverend Samuel May and his cousin, attorney Samuel E. Sewall, offered to help Garrison find subscribers for his newspaper.

By late December 1830, Garrison had gathered

$500 in advance from subscribers, both black and white, and finally had enough money to print the first edition of his paper. On January 1, 1831, he set the type for the first edition of *The Liberator*, a four-page newsletter printed on cheap paper with inexpensive ink, all he could afford. Even so, Garrison made sure his voice was heard, and the words he printed that day in *The Liberator* would become some of the most passionate words ever written against slavery:

> *I will be as harsh as truth, as uncompromising as justice. On this subject, I do not wish to think, or speak, or write, with moderation. No! No! Tell a man whose house is on fire to give a moderate alarm; tell him to moderately rescue his wife from the hands of the ravisher; tell the mother to gradually extricate her babe from the fire into which it has fallen—but urge me not to use moderation in a cause like the present.*

Garrison concluded his declaration with a statement that summed up his entire philosophy and drive to start an antislavery revolution:

> *I am in earnest—I will not equivocate—I will not excuse—I will not retreat a single inch—AND I WILL BE HEARD.*

JOHN QUINCY ADAMS.
HENRY WARD BEECHER.
WILLIAM LLOYD GARRISON.
JOHN GREENLEAF WHITTIER.
WILLIAM CULLEN BRYANT.
JOSHUA R. GIDDINGS.
WENDELL PHILLIPS.
CHARLES SUMNER.
GERRIT SMITH.
CASSIUS M. CLAY.
OWEN LOVEJOY.
BENJAMIN LUNDY.
Engraved by J.C. Buttre, New York.
EMINENT OPPONENTS OF THE SLAVE POWER.

Chapter 6 The Liberator

As he promised in the first issue of his newspaper, Garrison was heard. He enjoyed his new fame and saw himself as a reformer of all people. He didn't fear the harsh words of his critics, nor violence from those that threatened him, nor more jail time. His biggest fear, in fact, was not being heard.

Garrison found a small office and worked all day and into the night, often composing his stories directly on the typesetting box. He gave away many free copies, and even boldly mailed some to the South. And when editors at Southern papers got a hold of *The Liberator*, they attacked Garrison in the press. This made Garrison even happier; his word was being spread among the very people he was criticizing—for free!

Portraits representing some of the most prominent abolitionists of the 19th century, including William Lloyd Garrison

On August 22, 1831, a slave named Nat Turner led a two-day uprising in Virginia that left 57 white people dead, including the family of Joseph Travis, Turner's owner. Southern slave owners feared this act would spark a black revolution and sought to crush it as quickly as possible. Turner was eventually hanged, and more than 100 other slaves were beaten and killed. Weeks of violence and bloodshed followed the incident. Stricter laws were also passed against slaves and freed blacks.

Although he opposed violence and still believed in the possibility of a peaceful solution to end slavery, Garrison praised Turner in the pages of *The Liberator* for his courage.

Nat Turner was a black slave and preacher who led the most famous slave revolt in U.S. history. More whites died during the 1831 rebellion led by Turner than in any other slave revolt in the nation's history. Turner narrated a lengthy confession before he was hanged on November 11, 1831, at the age of 31.

I do not justify the slaves in their rebellion, yet I do not condemn them and applaud similar conduct in white men … Of all men living, however, our slaves have the best reason to assert their rights by violent measures, inasmuch as they are more oppressed than others.

There was no evidence that Turner had read any articles Garrison had written, but many Southerners blamed Garrison for

Nat Turner eluded capture for two months following the uprising until he was caught by a local farmer.

encouraging the bloody revolt. In Columbia, South Carolina, the Vigilance Committee offered $1,500 for the capture of anyone in possession of Garrison's newspaper. Other cities passed laws forbidding copies of *The Liberator* from leaving the post office.

Raleigh, North Carolina, blamed Garrison for provoking the slave revolts and promised to throw him in jail if he entered the city. The Georgia House of Representatives passed a bill that offered a $5,000 reward to anyone who could capture Garrison and bring him to court.

Garrison also received hundreds of letters threatening his life, but he wasn't deterred. Every threat, every harsh word against him made him feel more powerful than before. And each threat made Garrison's supporters even more devoted to the anti-slavery cause.

At the same time, Garrison had begun writing letters to British abolitionists, who had been suc-

In the mid-1800s, British antislavery societies packed meeting halls in London.

cessfully wiping out slavery in the British Empire. They told Garrison that a newspaper alone couldn't keep the antislavery revolution going. It needed large abolitionist societies that could organize public speeches, organize boycotts of slave-produced goods, and support politicians who opposed slavery. Garrison decided that Boston was ready for an antislavery organization, and he was going to start it.

But there was a problem. Many abolitionists already belonged to a group called the American Colonization Society, which believed that slaves should be freed and resettled in West Africa. The group seemed to agree with Garrison's idea that blacks should have their freedom, and he had briefly joined the group back in 1830, but Garrison soon realized that most members of the group didn't care as much about the blacks' well-being as they did reducing the number of free blacks in America. In less than a year, Garrison left the organization.

Garrison needed to convince members of the society to join his own antislavery organization. He published a book called *Thoughts on African Colonization*, in which he blasted supporters of colonization movement. The rate at which slaves were being purchased out of freedom and returned to Africa, he said, was painstakingly slow; the society had freed fewer than 2,000 slaves in 10 years. This process simply wouldn't work in a country with

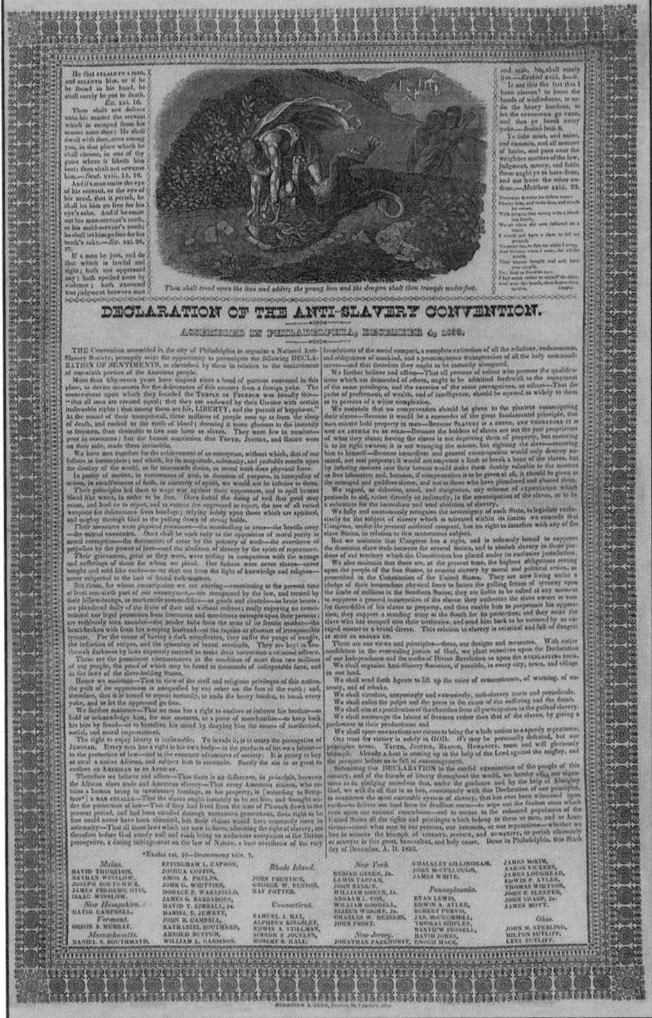

DECLARATION OF THE ANTI-SLAVERY CONVENTION.

ASSEMBLED IN PHILADELPHIA, DECEMBER 4, 1833.

A year after Garrison created the New England Anti-Slavery Society, 60 abolitionist leaders, including Garrison, created a national organization. Their declaration stated that members would work to free the slaves through non-violent actions.

two million slaves. Garrison also quickly learned that three-fourths of the American Colonization Society's officers owned slaves themselves. The president of the group owned 1,000. How, Garrison wondered, could someone truly care about freeing the slaves but also own them? It didn't make sense. Garrison then said that anyone who didn't care enough about slaves to support their immediate release, even if he didn't own slaves, was not much better than a slave owner. This bold statement damaged Garrison's popularity among would-be members of his new organization.

The goal of the New England Anti-Slavery Society was to bring about the abolition of slavery in the United States. The Society sought to improve the lives of blacks, to educate the public about their plight, and to obtain for blacks equal civil and political rights with whites.

Finally, he convinced a few people to attend a meeting. On a cold night in January 1832, 15 abolitionists assembled at the African Meeting House in Boston. The New England Anti-Slavery Society was born.

AMERICAN ANTI-SLAVERY ALMANAC,

FOR

1840,

BEING BISSEXTILE OR LEAP-YEAR, AND THE 64TH OF AMERICAN INDEPENDENCE. CALCULATED FOR NEW YORK; ADAPTED TO THE NORTHERN AND MIDDLE STATES.

NORTHERN HOSPITALITY—NEW YORK NINE MONTHS' LAW.

The slave steps out of the slave-state, and his chains fall. A free state, with another chain, stands ready to re-enslave him.

Thus saith the Lord, Deliver him that is spoiled out of the hands of the oppressor.

NEW YORK:

PUBLISHED BY THE AMERICAN ANTI-SLAVERY SOCIETY,

NO. 143 NASSAU STREET.

Chapter 7 Riot in Boston

At the center of the New England Anti-Slavery Society's beliefs was the idea of immediate emancipation, that all slaves should be given their freedom without delay. Although his band of believers was few in number, Garrison saw the society as a force that would spread throughout the country until it was so large and powerful that it would wipe out slavery forever. He predicted victory by 1840, and while he was wrong about the end of slavery, he was right about the growth of his organization. By the end of the decade, there would be more than 2,000 abolitionist societies with 250,000 members across the United States.

The attacks against Garrison became more frequent and severe. People threw rotten eggs at him

The American Anti-Slavery Society, of which Garrison was a member, encouraged public lectures, boycotts of slave-produced goods, and antislavery publications such as this almanac.

when he spoke in public. He was greeted with rocks when he left his office. One morning, he awoke to find a wooden gallows constructed on his lawn. It was well known that if Garrison set foot in a Southern state, he would almost certainly be murdered. Still, Garrison insisted that he didn't fear for his safety. He was doing God's work, he said, and God would protect him.

Although he was a "madman" in print, in person Garrison resembled a gentle schoolteacher, a comparison that was commonly made about the frail abolitionist. He wore small wire-rimmed glasses, and his wispy white hair failed to cover the top of his head. It was this strange difference between appearance and character that attracted Helen Benson, the sister of one of Garrison's abolitionist friends. And when Garrison met the young woman with "blue eyes and fair brown hair," he fell in love and asked for her hand in marriage. One of the many letters he sent her from Boston read:

> *Your humility charms me, and your good sense and wise judgment. I love [the] simplicity of dress, of manners, and of mind. Of course, I love* you.

On September 4, 1834, the couple married in a simple ceremony at Helen's family home in Connecticut. The Reverend Samuel J. May, the very

Garrison (center) often met with fellow abolitionists George Thompson (left) and Wendell Phillips (right) to discuss ways to end slavery.

same man who had helped Garrison raise money for *The Liberator*, presided over the wedding.

The newlyweds moved into a small cottage in Roxbury, Massachusetts, about three miles (5 km) from Boston. Each night, Garrison would make the walk home from his office alone—an unwise move, considering the many enemies he had made. One night, he noticed two shadowy figures armed with clubs trailing behind him. He continued toward home, and they followed but kept their distance.

The next night he noticed the same pair following him again. Garrison asked people around town about the figures and discovered that the men were actually bodyguards hired by Boston's black community to protect him. Fearing for the safety of his wife, Garrison decided to move back to Boston.

English politician George Thompson played a role in passing the Emancipation Act of 1834, which was the first step in abolishing slavery in all British colonies.

In the spring of 1835, Garrison invited the leader of the London Anti-Slavery Society, George Thompson, to come to America and speak about the successes of abolitionism in the British colonies. Both men shared very similar ideas about ending slavery and had led similar lives, and neither feared any reaction to their teaming up in America. But they never anticipated a riot.

That summer, Thompson traveled around New England speaking at antislavery meetings. Like Garrison, he was a fearless speaker, and he didn't hesitate to pass judgment on anyone who didn't agree with his views. And like Garrison, Thompson earned more enemies than friends with bold and controversial speeches. More than once he narrowly escaped an angry mob.

In October, *The Liberator* advertised that Garrison and Thompson would speak in front of the Boston Female Anti-Slavery Society. Before the address, a note was slipped under the door of Garrison's office, promising both men that they would be covered in tar and feathers if they ever published their paper again. Another letter notified them of a $100 reward for the first person to attack Thompson. Garrison wasn't worried about his own safety but was concerned about his friend. He urged Thompson to leave the city, and he did so. Garrison, however, would give the speech as planned.

By the time he arrived for his speech, a crowd of about 100 men was already standing around outside. It was clear these men weren't members of the Society, but Garrison remained steadfast and entered the auditorium. Just as the meeting began, Theodore

Like Garrison, English abolitionist George Thompson angered many people with his antislavery views. Members of a pro-slavery group once planned to capture him after a speaking engagement in Boston, ship him to South Carolina, and lynch him. After Thompson's speech, a group of about 30 abolitionists clustered around him, asking questions. While Thompson talked with them, they gradually moved him toward a rear door through which he escaped to an awaiting carriage. The pro-slavery group had no idea that Thompson had left the hall.

Lyman, the mayor of Boston, accompanied by police officers, burst in. He ordered the women to go home and warned the crowd of the violence that would occur if they didn't comply. The women formed a line and marched outside, where the angry mob parted and let them go on their way. Garrison, however, remained inside the building.

Once the mob realized Garrison had not come out, they charged into the building to cries of "Let's get Garrison!" but the outspoken crusader was nowhere to be seen. The men searched the auditorium and the surrounding buildings and eventually found Garrison hiding behind a pile of lumber in a carpenter's shop.

If someone is lynched, he or she is killed, generally by hanging, by a mob in defiance of law and order. Victims of a lynching do not have a chance to defend themselves. The mob assumes its victims are guilty, whether or not the victims have had a trial. Lynch mobs not only promote disrespect for law, order, and basic human rights, they also encourage mass brutality.

They tied a rope around Garrison's waist and dragged him out of the shop and into the street. "Lynch him!" they cried. "Lynch Garrison!" The mob surrounded their captive, cursed him, and spit on him. But Garrison didn't struggle, nor did he show signs of fear. He remained calm, accepting whatever was to come.

Mayor Lyman ordered brothers Daniel and Aaron Cooley to

rescue the abolitionist. They pushed their way through the angry mob, grabbed Garrison, and rushed him to City Hall. The mayor offered Garrison protection; if he would plead guilty to disturbing the

REPORT

OF THE

BOSTON FEMALE

ANTI SLAVERY SOCIETY;

WITH A CONCISE

STATEMENT OF EVENTS,

PREVIOUS AND SUBSEQUENT TO THE

ANNUAL MEETING OF 1835.

BOSTON:
PUBLISHED BY THE SOCIETY.

1836.

The title page of a meeting report from the Boston Female Anti-Slavery Society, founded in1834 by 12 women, including sisters Maria, Caroline, Anne, and Deborah Weston

Garrison showed no fear despite the hostile mob that dragged him through the streets of Boston in 1835.

peace, Garrison could spend the night in jail, where he would be safe. Garrison agreed, knowing that if he went back outside, the mob would certainly capture him again and possibly hang him.

Garrison woke up in his cell the next morning and scratched the following into the wall:

> *Wm. Lloyd Garrison was put into this cell Wednesday afternoon, October 21, 1835, to save him from the violence of a 'respectable and influential' mob, who sought to destroy him for preaching the*

abominable and dangerous doctrine that 'all men are created equal,' and that all oppression is odious [hateful] in the sight of God ... Reader, let this inscription remain till the last slave in this despotic land be loosed from his fetters [shackles].

These words would remain etched in the wall for 17 years, at which time the jail was torn down. Unfortunately, it would still be many years before the last slave walked free.

Chapter 8 Dividing the Nation

Despite the hostility he faced from pro-slavery groups, Garrison continued to preach against the evils of slavery throughout the late 1830s and early 1840s. In 1841, he met Frederick Douglass, a man who would help him rise to the frontlines of the fight against slavery.

Although Garrison was an intense man when writing or speaking against slavery, he was a gentle father and husband at home, which surprised even his closest antislavery friends. They knew Garrison the lion, the intense editor, and champion of the abolitionist cause. They didn't know Garrison the mild family man. Garrison and his wife, Helen, eventually had seven children: George, William Jr., Wendell, Charles, Helen, Elizabeth, and Francis.

Like Garrison, former slave Frederick Douglass spread his abolitionist message through public speeches and publications.

Garrison also displayed tenderness to his long-lost brother when he showed up at the Garrison home unexpectedly. Although James had deserted his family years before, Garrison welcomed him back with open arms. James asked his brother for help in avoiding the "demon rum" and promised he would never drink again. Garrison hoped James was telling the truth.

But James soon faltered. He took a trip to Canada to seek out members of his father's family but instead found only his father's old vice: alcohol. Garrison cared for his brother when he returned to Boston, but James's health diminished quickly, and he died in September 1842.

When not attending to his young family, Garrison continued fighting slavery with words, both in *The Liberator* and at public addresses, which he delivered with more frequency. Although he still didn't have a plan, Garrison pressed on for slaves to be given their immediate freedom. By 1840, his influence in the North was evident. He had helped many people change their thinking about slavery. Antislavery organizations were becoming larger and more powerful; even politicians who would have dodged the slavery question in the past were taking a stand and supporting emancipation.

But many who were opposed to slavery still didn't agree with all of Garrison's ideas. For one, he

Garrison's children continued their father's work for women's rights into the early 1900s through organizations such as the New England Women's Club, pictured here.

believed in equal rights for *all* people and was a strict supporter of women's rights, while many men—even the clergy—still believed that a woman's place was at home. Even though he was very religious himself, Garrison attacked organized religion for not fighting slavery more aggressively. He also thought that slavery shouldn't be just a political issue. Slavery was an issue that went far beyond politics, and he feared that antislavery societies would use the slavery issue to further their own political candidates and agendas. So Garrison

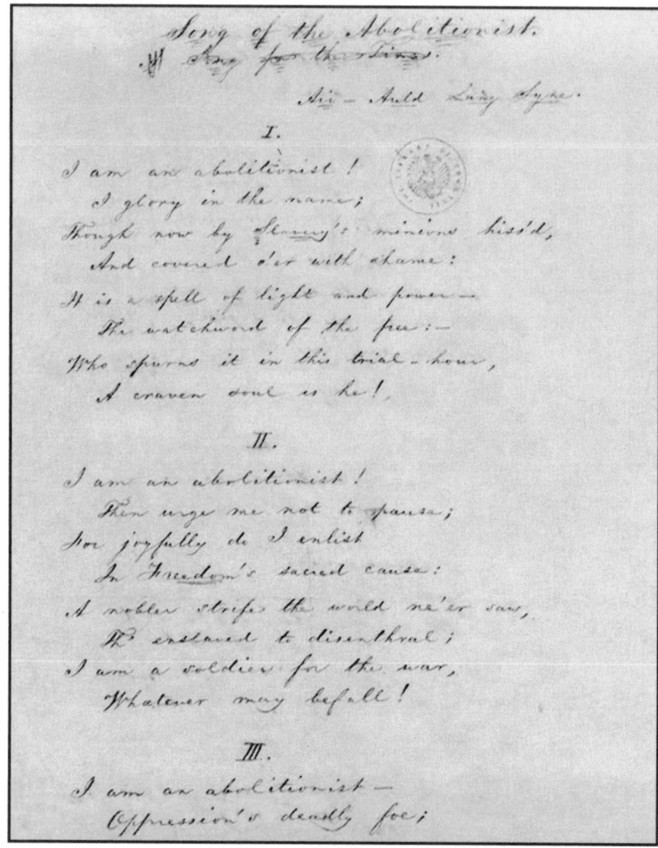
Song of the Abolitionist.

~~A Song for the Times.~~

Air — Auld Lang Syne.

I.

I am an abolitionist!
I glory in the name;
Though now by Slavery's minions hiss'd,
And covered o'er with shame:
It is a spell of light and power —
The watchword of the free:—
Who spurns it in this trial-hour,
A craven soul is he!

II.

I am an abolitionist!
Then urge me not to pause;
For joyfully do I enlist
In Freedom's sacred cause:
A nobler strife the world ne'er saw,
Th' enslaved to disenthral;
I am a soldier for the war,
Whatever may befall!

III.

I am an abolitionist —
Oppression's deadly foe;

Garrison wrote his antislavery poem "Song of the Abolitionist" in 1841.

refused to endorse, or support, any politician.

This unwillingness to work with the government angered many of Garrison's followers. They broke off from the American Anti-Slavery Society and formed their own organizations. Votes were the key to ending slavery, they said, and they found and backed politicians who would support their cause in the U.S. Congress. Garrison had little faith in politicians, believing that they gave up their sense of right and wrong as soon as they took office. Garrison was losing power within his own movement.

In 1841, Garrison took a vacation to the small island of Nantucket off the coast of Massachusetts. But the restless abolitionist couldn't relax while countless slaves were still being treated like animals. He had heard about an escaped slave in the nearby town of New Bedford, a self-taught and hardworking man who spent some of his meager earnings on a subscription to *The Liberator*.

When Garrison met Douglass, the former slave told him that he agreed with Garrison's attacks on organized religion. "Those ministers who defend slavery from the Bible are of their 'father and devil,'" he said. "And those churches that regard slaveholders as Christians are synagogues of Satan. In fact, Mr. Garrison, our nation is a nation of liars!" Douglass told Garrison about his experiences as a slave: the whippings, the lack of food and shelter, and the ways in which masters mistreated their women slaves. Garrison was devastated by the account, and he demanded that Douglass tell

Frederick Douglass was born February 7, 1817, in Tuckahoe, Maryland. He escaped from his master when he was a young man and worked many odd jobs until he found his calling as a speaker on the subject of slavery. Douglass also became a noted social reformer and author. He devoted his life to the abolition of slavery and fighting for the rights of blacks.

other white people about his wretched past, so they could hear for themselves what it was like to live the life of a slave.

Garrison arranged to have Douglass speak in front of a crowd of white abolitionists. Douglass repeated the stories he had told Garrison, telling them about the cruelties he had seen and suffered.

Many of the abolitionists had never heard a former slave tell his story before, and the group was greatly moved by the speech. When Douglass finished, Garrison grabbed the opportunity to excite the visibly shaken crowd. "Have we been listening to a thing, a piece of property, or to a man?" Garrison asked.

"A man!" the crowd shouted.

"And should such a man be held a slave in a republican or Christian land?" he challenged.

"Never! Never!" they cried.

"Shall such a man ever be sent back to slavery from the soil of old Massachusetts?"

"No! No! No!"

Douglass was instantly famous. He continued to speak all over New England on behalf of slaves. He wrote a book called the *Narrative of the Life of Frederick Douglass, An American Slave*, which was widely read. The book taught many Northern whites, those who had never witnessed slavery, that the practice was indeed evil.

Being tied to a whipping post and beaten was just one of the many brutalities endured by slaves in the United States during the 19th century.

Even though *The Liberator* was barely making enough money to stay alive, Garrison kept publishing, and he added more evils to his list of targets. He spoke out against war and called his readers hypocrites for electing military presidents. He continued to attack various social ills, including smoking, drinking, and cruelty to animals, and

Garrison published this poem in 1849 in a special section of The Liberator that targeted women readers.

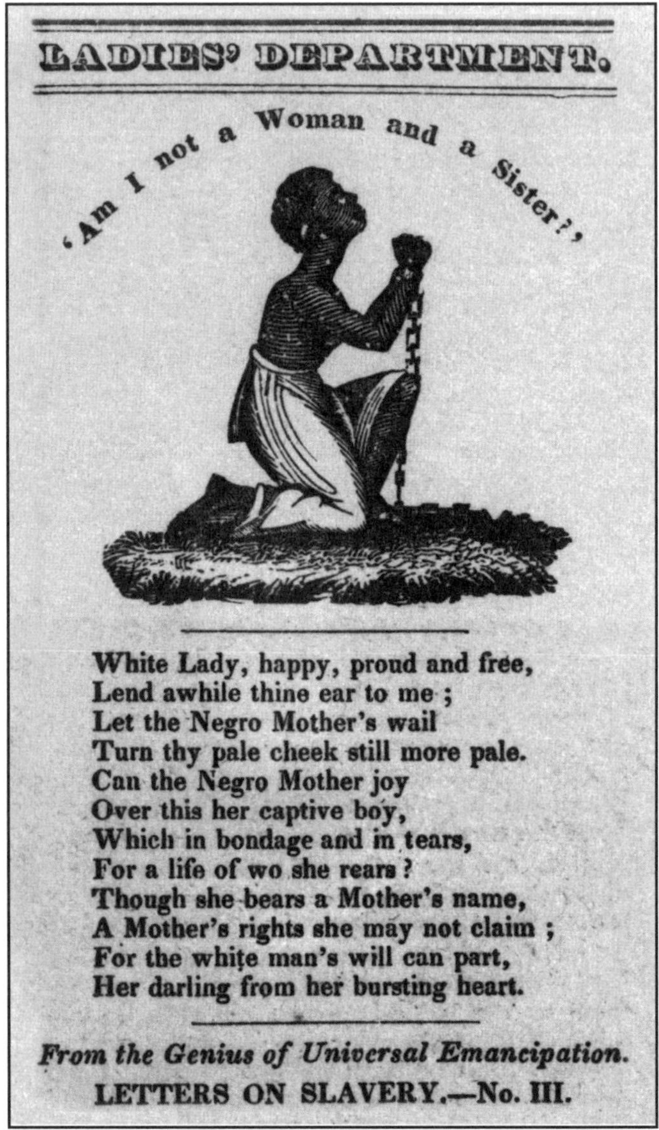

LADIES' DEPARTMENT.

White Lady, happy, proud and free,
Lend awhile thine ear to me ;
Let the Negro Mother's wail
Turn thy pale cheek still more pale.
Can the Negro Mother joy
Over this her captive boy,
Which in bondage and in tears,
For a life of wo she rears ?
Though she bears a Mother's name,
A Mother's rights she may not claim ;
For the white man's will can part,
Her darling from her bursting heart.

From the Genius of Universal Emancipation.

LETTERS ON SLAVERY.—No. III.

fought discrimination against women.

But by 1845, Garrison had been preaching against these things for years with few positive results. He was discouraged and wondered if there ever could be a solution to slavery that Northerners would adopt. He turned to his Bible for help and found this passage from the book of Isaiah: "We have made a covenant with death, and with hell we are in agreement."

"Of course!" Garrison said to himself. By upholding the U.S. Constitution, which permitted slavery, the North was in a covenant with the South to make property out of other human beings. As long as both halves of the country were in the same Union, the American government was tolerating slavery. If the Declaration of Independence said that all men are created equal, then the Constitution should agree. Garrison saw only one solution to the problem, which he printed in big letters on the front page of *The Liberator:* "DISSOLUTION NOW." Garrison believed the North should secede, or break away, from the Union.

Garrison let his new plan of action be known at every speech he made. "No Union with slaveholders!" he cried at the meeting halls. "No Union!" Of course, many of his antislavery supporters thought this was too drastic of a solution. But by the 1850s, the idea of secession was being discussed across the country, in newspapers and churches, on street corners and public squares, and at the dinner table. Abolitionism was more widespread than ever in the North, thanks in part to a novel published in 1852 by a white woman named Harriet Beecher Stowe. Her book, *Uncle Tom's Cabin,* was about a religious slave who defies his masters to help his fellow slaves, ultimately at the cost of his own life.

The book had a tremendous impact all over America. In the North, Stowe had introduced even more people to the horrors of slavery. In the South, the novel sparked a furious backlash. Stowe became as hated as her friend Garrison.

Harriet Beecher Stowe was born on June 14, 1811, in Litchfield, Connecticut. Her father, Lyman Beecher, was a Presbyterian minister. Stowe was educated at the academy in Litchfield and at Hartford Female Seminary. From 1832 to 1850, she lived in Cincinnati, Ohio, where her father served as the president of Lane Theological Seminary. In 1836, she married Calvin Stowe, a member of the Lane faculty. Her years in Cincinnati inspired many of the characters and incidents in her novel Uncle Tom's Cabin.

At a Fourth of July rally in Framingham, Massachusetts, in 1854, a crowd of 3,000 people gathered to hear Garrison speak. At the end of his address, he held up a copy of the Constitution and claimed it to be the evil root of slavery. "This is the source and parent of all other atrocities," he said, and repeated the words he had pulled from the Bible. "A covenant with death and an agreement with hell!" He lit a match and set fire to the yellowed paper. It burst into flames. "So perish all compromises with tyranny!"

"Amen!" the crowd replied.

Potential buyers had the opportunity to inspect slaves prior to bidding on them at a slave auction.

During the 1850s, the U.S. government made several decisions that seemed to take a step back from ending slavery. Fearing secession by the South, Congress passed the Compromise of 1850, which allowed Texas to enter the Union as a slave state and California as a free state. Part of the Compromise was the Fugitive Slave Act, which held Northerners criminally responsible for aiding runaway slaves. In 1854, Congress passed the Kansas-Nebraska Act, which allowed states to decide for themselves whether to permit slavery. And in 1857, the Supreme Court ruled that slaves could not file

U.S. Marines storm the engine house at Harpers Ferry on October 18, 1859, after it had been captured by John Brown.

suit in a federal court because, as the court interpreted the Constitution, slaves were property and not people. This proved to Garrison that he was right: The Constitution was a pro-slavery document.

Each time an act was passed, Garrison fought back in *The Liberator* and in his public addresses. And unlike before, the majority of his followers now agreed with him. The North was unifying against slavery and, on a larger scale, against the South. Civil war seemed inevitable.

Although Garrison was strictly opposed to violence, many others had decided that force, perhaps even war, would be necessary to end slavery. In 1859, a farmer named John Brown, who had heard Garrison speak, gathered some men and seized the U.S. Arsenal and Armory at Harpers Ferry in present-day West Virginia. Brown had already killed five pro-slavery men in Kansas and planned on using the weapons he had captured to support a series of slave uprisings. But a company of U.S. Marines under the command of Colonel Robert E. Lee stopped Brown and his men before they could leave the armory. Ten of them were killed, and Brown was injured. Two months later he was hanged.

Despite his hatred of violence, Garrison praised Brown's courage in the pages of his newspaper. He felt sympathy for Brown and his "well-intentioned effort by insurrection to emancipate the slaves in Virginia." On the day Brown was hanged in Charlestown, Virginia, Garrison made a bold statement. If the country's forefathers had been justified in fighting for unfair taxation during the Revolutionary War, he said, Brown was even more justified for fighting against slavery. "In firing his gun," Garrison said, "John Brown has merely told us what time of day it is. It is high noon … thank God!" A civil war was coming, and even the most stubborn preacher of nonresistance had admitted it.

Chapter 9 Mission Accomplished

When Abraham Lincoln was elected president in 1860, it was the final push the South needed to secede from the Union. Lincoln had been nominated by the Republican Party, which was formed by the abolitionist politicians. But Lincoln had beat the South's nominee, Stephen A. Douglas, by only a few hundred thousand votes—not a large margin. The South refused to live under an abolitionist president, and in December 1860, some states officially seceded from the Union—the very same thing Garrison had been urging the North to do for years.

Garrison had not voted for Lincoln—he still believed that ending slavery should not be a political cause—but he had encouraged others to do so. After Lincoln was elected, Garrison wrote to the new

Abraham Lincoln was sworn into office as president of the United States on March 4, 1861.

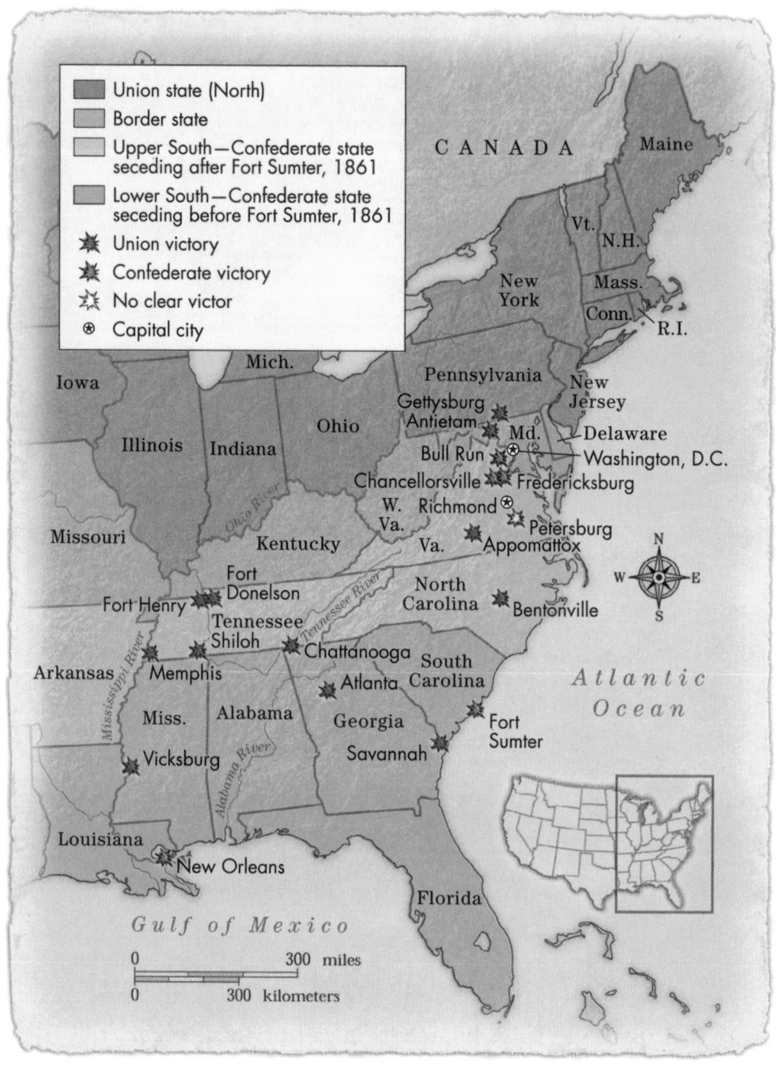

Most battles of the Civil War were fought in the South.

president. He wanted Lincoln to tell the South good riddance. Let them organize their own league of states, he said. Let them break away so the North could be free of their evil ways!

The Civil War officially began when the

Confederate Army captured Fort Sumter in South Carolina in April 1861. This put Garrison in a personal dilemma: For years he had been preaching against violence, politics, and the evil of slavery. Now, he was supporting a violent war and a political figure—Abraham Lincoln. But Garrison believed that the war would be the quickest route to an end of slavery. He told the New England Anti-Slavery Society that he wholeheartedly believed in the Northern cause.

Many of Garrison's supporters were surprised by his change of character. He explained his new position at a meeting in New York, saying he had made bold statements in the past under the assumption that things would never change:

> *When I said I would die a bachelor, I did not think I should live till I were married. And when I said I would not sustain the Constitution because it was a covenant with death and an agreement with hell, I had not idea that I should live to see death and hell secede!*

Abraham Lincoln was the 16th president of the United States. The son of a Kentucky frontiersman, Lincoln didn't have the advantage of a formal education, so he made extraordinary efforts to attain knowledge on his own while he worked on a farm, split rails for fences, and ran a store in New Salem, Illinois. Lincoln grew into one of the truly great men of all time, leading the country through its greatest crisis to date, the Civil War (1861–1865).

With the Civil War underway, Garrison seemed to calm down. He finally felt assured that slavery would soon come to an end. On January 1, 1863, Lincoln issued the Emancipation Proclamation, a document declaring free any slaves living in states that weren't under Union control—namely, the Southern states that had seceded. But the carefully worded Emancipation didn't actually free any slaves, because the Union couldn't enforce the proclamation in the states outside of its control. However, the document helped shift the goals of the Civil War toward the ultimate goal of ending slavery throughout the entire United States.

On February 1, 1865, the Union achieved that goal when Congress approved the 13th Amendment to the Constitution, officially ending slavery throughout the nation. When the Civil War ended in April, the seceded states were required to sign the new amendment before they could become part of the United States once again.

The Liberator's headline declared its editor's joy: "Hallelujah! Praise be to God!" Now that the slaves were free, there wasn't much use for Garrison's paper. In December 1865, Garrison published his last issue. He thanked his readers for their support, acknowledging the difficulties the paper had faced to deliver its antislavery message.

This engraving from 1865 celebrates the emancipation of the slaves following the Civil War.

I began publication of The Liberator *without a subscriber, and I end it … without a farthing as a … result of the patronage extended to it during thirty-five years of unremitted labors. From the immense change wrought in the national feeling and sentiment on the subject of slavery,* The Liberator *derived no advantage at any time in regard to its circulation.*

Garrison's antislavery work was done.

Chapter 10 Rest at Last

Garrison was almost 60 years old when he could finally say that his life's work was a success. By the end of the war, he was ready to settle down and enjoy his fame and the recognition of his peers. During his career, Garrison had spent all of his money on the abolitionist cause and his newspaper, and he retired virtually penniless. But a group of his friends and supporters raised $31,000 to ensure that Garrison could retire comfortably. One memorable contribution came from a former slave who donated $1 and wrote, "If I were a millionaire by the God's I would give him $1,000,000 & make him President of the United States. When he dies his destiny is the Heaven of Heavens."

Many of Garrison's former foes—abolitionists

William Lloyd Garrison circa 1865

who had believed his ideas too radical—became his admirers, and he accepted them with open arms. At an event celebrating the 13th Amendment he acknowledged this shift in opinion, saying, "I am unspeakably happy to believe that the great mass of my countrymen are now heartily disposed to admit that I have not acted the part of a madman, fanatic, incendiary or traitor."

Garrison continued to receive thanks and praise everywhere he went. Soon after the war, he visited Charleston, South Carolina, and was greeted by thousands of former slaves. He visited the Zion Church, where the newly freed black citizens lifted Garrison up on their shoulders and paraded him through the streets. A freed slave named Samuel Dickerson introduced Garrison to his two young daughters, who had been taken away from him into slavery but were now reunited. "I have read of you. I have read of your mighty labors ... and here is your handiwork," Dickerson said, referring to the girls. "Through your instrumentality, under the folds of that glorious flag ... you have restored them to me."

The 13th Amendment to the Constitution bans slavery within the United States and its territories, stating that "neither slavery nor involuntary servitude, except as a punishment for crime whereof the party shall have been duly convicted, shall exist within the United States, or any place subject to their jurisdiction." It also says that Congress has the power to enforce this law.

Soon after his visit to Charleston, Garrison received the news that President Lincoln had been shot and killed. Garrison was shocked. Although he had often criticized Lincoln for not moving quickly enough to end slavery, he respected the man and knew that if Lincoln had not been elected, slavery might still be legal in the United States.

In his remaining years, Garrison delivered the occasional lecture and remained an advocate for women's rights and justice for Native Americans. He also helped run an organization to improve education for blacks.

Garrison's wife died in 1876. After the burial, he left Boston to live with his daughter Helen Frances (Fanny) in New York, where he spent his final years. In May 1879, when he was almost 75 years old, his doctor diagnosed him with bladder and kidney trouble. Surrounded by his children, Garrison died at Fanny's home on May 24.

On the evening of April 14, 1865, Abraham Lincoln attended a performance at Ford's Theatre in Washington, D.C. Shortly after 10:00 P.M., he was shot in the head by John Wilkes Booth. Booth broke his leg as he leapt down to the stage from the presidential viewing box but limped across the stage, pursued by officials, waving a dagger and crying, "Sic semper tyrannis!" ("Thus always to tyrants!") Lincoln was carried unconscious to a neighboring house, where he died the following morning.

More than 70 newspapers throughout the United

Hate groups such as the Ku Klux Klan terrorized blacks long after the Civil War ended.

States and Europe published tributes to the deceased abolitionist. At his funeral, most people referred to Garrison's role in the antislavery movement, quoting the his own words from past issues of

The Liberator. Wendell Phillips, however, an abolitionist whom Garrison had mentored and for whom one of Garrison's sons was named, chose to speak about Garrison's personal life:

> *His was the happiest life I ever saw. No need for pity. No man gathered into his bosom a fuller sheaf of blessing, delight, and joy ... Every one of his near friends will agree with me that this was the happiest life God has granted in our day to any American standing in the foremost rank of influence and effort.*

Later that day, free blacks in cities across the United States met and prayed for Garrison—the stubborn man who had fought so long and so tirelessly for their freedom.

Garrison's Life

1805

William Lloyd Garrison is born in Newburyport, Massachusetts

1815

Moves to Baltimore, Maryland, with his mother and brother; becomes a shoemaker's apprentice

1817

Becomes a cabinetmaker's apprentice in Haverhill, Massachusetts

1805

1809

Louis Braille of France, inventor of a writing system for the blind, is born

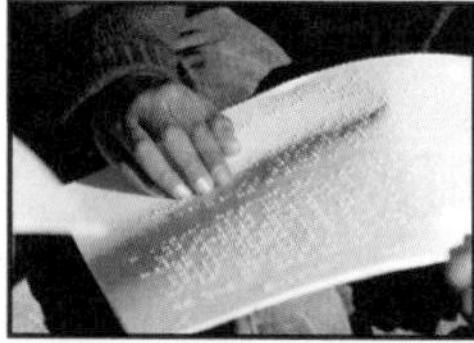

1814-1815

European states meet in Vienna, Austria, to redraw national borders after the conclusion of the Napoleonic Wars

World Events

1819

Starts his apprenticeship at the *Newburyport Herald*

1821

Writes his first article as "An Old Bachelor" in the *Herald*

1826

Buys *The Free Press* in Newburyport; folds his business the same year

1820

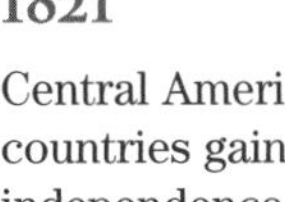

1821

Central American countries gain independence from Spain

1826

The first photograph is taken by Joseph Niépce, a French physicist

Garrison's Life

1827

Hired as the editor of Boston's *National Philanthropist*

1829

September 8, publishes the first edition of the *Genius of Universal Emancipation* with Benjamin Lundy

1830

Found guilty of libel; serves six months in the Baltimore city jail

1830

World Events

1827

Modern-day matches are invented by coating the end of a wooden stick with phosphorus

1829

The first practical sewing machine is invented by French tailor Barthélemy Thimonnier

1834

September 4, marries Helen Benson

1835

October 21, causes a riot and is dragged through the streets of Boston

1831

January 1, publishes the first edition of *The Liberator*

1835

1833

Great Britain abolishes slavery

Garrison's Life

1836
Son George Thompson is born, the first of seven Garrison children

1841
Meets Frederick Douglass, a former slave

1854
Burns a copy of the U.S. Constitution at an antislavery rally

1850

1836
Texans defeat Mexican troops at San Jacinto after a deadly battle at the Alamo

1848
The Communist Manifesto by German writer Karl Marx is widely distributed

World Events

1865

Publishes the last edition of *The Liberator* after the Civil War ends

1879

May 24, dies in New York at his daughter Fanny's home

1860

The South secedes from the Union, eventually leading to the American Civil War

1865

1865

Lewis Carroll writes *Alice's Adventures in Wonderland*

1877

German inventor Nikolaus A. Otto works on what will become the internal combustion engine for automobiles

Life at a Glance

Date of Birth:	December 12, 1805
Birthplace:	Newburyport, Massachusetts
Father:	Abijah Garrison (1773–after 1814)
Mother:	Francis (Fanny) Maria Lloyd (1776–1823)
Siblings:	Maria, Caroline, James
Education:	Some grammar school
Spouse:	Helen Benson (1811–1876)
Date of Marriage:	September 4, 1834
Children:	George (1836–1904), William Jr. (1838–1909), Wendell (1840–1907), Charles (1842–1849), Helen (1844–1928), Elizabeth (1846–1848), Francis (1848–1916)
Date of Death:	May 24, 1879
Place of Burial:	Roxbury, Massachusetts

Additional Resources

In the Library

De Capua, Sarah. *Abolitionists: A Force for Change.* Chanhassen, Minn.: The Child's World, 2002.

January, Brendan. *John Brown's Raid on Harpers Ferry.* New York: Children's Press, 2000.

Landau, Elaine. *The Abolitionist Movement.* New York: Children's Press, 2004.

Lawing, Charles B. *William Lloyd Garrison and the Liberator.* Greensboro, N.C.: Morgan Reynolds Publishing, 2001.

Lowance, Mason. *Against Slavery: An Abolitionist Reader.* New York: Penguin Books, 2000.

Lutz, Norma Jean, and Arthur M. Schlesinger Jr. *Frederick Douglass: Abolitionist and Author.* Langhorne, Pa.: Chelsea House Publishers, 2001.

On the Web

For more information on *William Lloyd Garrison*, use FactHound to track down Web sites related to this book.

1. Go to *www.facthound.com*
2. Type in a search word related to this book or this book ID: 0756508193
3. Click on the *Fetch It* button.

FactHound will find the best Web sites for you.

Historic Sites

Greater Newburyport
Chamber of Commerce & Industry
38R Merrimac Street
Newburyport, MA 01950
978/462-6680
www.newburyportchamber.org
To explore the hometown of William Lloyd Garrison

United States National Slavery Museum
1320 Central Park Boulevard, Suite 251
Fredericksburg, VA 22401
540/548-8818
www.usnationalslaverymuseum.org
OPEN IN 2007: To learn about the history of slavery in America

abolitionists
people who are against slavery and fight to end it

advocates
people who urge support for something they believe in

apprenticeship
a stated amount of time during which a person is legally bound to learn a trade or an art from another who is experienced in that field

boycott
a refusal to buy certain goods or services as a form of protest

controversial
something that a lot of people disagree about

destiny
a series of events that are believed to be determined in advance

emancipation
freedom from slavery

Federalist Party
a group of early Americans who wanted a strong federal government

gallows
two upright posts with a third post sideways between them; used to hang people

hypocrite
a person who believes in rules he doesn't follow

journalism
writing and editing for a newspaper or magazine

legislation
rules that become law after being voted on by lawmakers

libel
saying or writing something about someone that isn't true

lynch
to kill someone, usually by hanging, without first giving him or her a trial

oppression
unfair use of power over someone

prophecy
the telling of something before it happens

social reformer
someone who works to make society better for everyone

vices
bad habits, such as drinking alcohol or gambling

Chapter 1

Page 11, line 1: Walter M. Merrill. *Against Wind and Tide: A Biography of Wm. Lloyd Garrison.* Cambridge, Mass.: Harvard University Press, 1963, pp. 7–8.

Chapter 3

Page 25, line 15: Doris Faber. *I Will Be Heard: The Life of William Lloyd Garrison.* New York: Lothrop, Lee and Shepard Company, 1970, p. 27.

Page 27, line 4: Jules Archer. *Angry Abolitionist: William Lloyd Garrison.* New York: Julian Messner, 1969, p. 18.

Page 29, line 3: Ibid., p. 19.

Chapter 4

Page 40, line 1: Ibid., p. 27.

Page 42, line 13: *I Will Be Heard: The Life of William Lloyd Garrison* (Faber), p. 50.

Chapter 5

Page 47, line 3: Ibid., pp. 55–56.

Page 49, line 27: Henry Mayer. *All on Fire: William Lloyd Garrison and the Abolition of Slavery.* New York: St. Martin's Press, 1998, p. 102.

Page 51, line 10: Ibid., p. 112.

Page 51, line 26: Ibid., p. 112.

Chapter 6

Page 54, line 14: *Angry Abolitionist: William Lloyd Garrison* (Archer), p. 50.

Chapter 7

Page 62, line 21: Ibid., pp. 73–74.

Page 68, line 8: Ibid., p. 90.

Chapter 8

Page 75, line 15: Frederick Douglass. *Narrative of the Life of Frederick Douglass, An American Slave.* New York: Barnes & Noble, 2003, pp. 1–11.

Page 80, line 18: *Against Wind and Tide: A Biography of Wm. Lloyd Garrison* (Merrill), p. 268.

Page 83, line 17: *All on Fire: William Lloyd Garrison and the Abolition of Slavery* (Mayer), p. 494.

Page 83, line 24: *I Will Be Heard: The Life of William Lloyd Garrison* (Faber), p. 107.

Chapter 9

Page 87, line 19: Ibid., p. 109.

Page 89, line 1: *Angry Abolitionist: William Lloyd Garrison* (Archer), p. 171.

Chapter 10

Page 92, line 21: *All on Fire: William Lloyd Garrison and the Abolition of Slavery* (Mayer), p. 583.

Page 92, sidebar: 13th Amendment to the U.S. Constitution.

Page 95, line 6: Harriet Hyman Alonso. *Growing Up Abolitionist: The Story of the Garrison Children.* Amherst, Mass.: University of Massachusetts Press, 2002, p. 254.

Select Bibliography

Alonso, Harriet Hyman. *Growing Up Abolitionist: The Story of the Garrison Children.* Amherst, Mass.: University of Massachusetts Press, 2002.

Archer, Jules. *Angry Abolitionist: William Lloyd Garrison.* New York: Julian Messner, 1969.

Douglass, Frederick. *Narrative of the Life of Frederick Douglass, An American Slave.* New York: Barnes & Noble, 2003.

Faber, Doris. *I Will Be Heard: The Life of William Lloyd Garrison.* New York: Lothrop, Lee and Shepard Company, 1970.

Jacobs, Donald M., ed. *Courage and Conscience: Black & White Abolitionists in Boston.* Bloomington, Ind.: Indiana University Press, 1993.

Mayer, Henry. *All on Fire: William Lloyd Garrison and the Abolition of Slavery.* New York: St. Martin's Press, 1998.

Merrill, Walter M. *Against Wind and Tide: A Biography of Wm. Lloyd Garrison.* Cambridge, Mass.: Harvard University Press, 1963.

Steward, James Brewer. *William Lloyd Garrison and the Challenge of Emancipation.* Arlington Heights, Ill.: Harlan Davidson Inc., 1992.

Index

Index

About the Author

Nick Fauchald lives and writes in New York City. A native of Red Wing, Minnesota, he attended St. Olaf College in Northfield, Minnesota. This is his seventh children's book.

Image Credits

Herbert Orth/Time Life Pictures/Getty Images, cover (top), 4–5, 68–69, 99 (top right); Stock Montage/Getty Images, cover (bottom), 2; North Wind Picture Archives, 8, 12, 14, 20, 22, 24, 27, 28, 32, 44, 55, 63, 81, 96 (top right), 99 (top left); Hulton Archive/Getty Images, 11, 43, 56, 64, 94, 97; Stock Montage, 17, 39, 96 (top left), 98 (top); Bettmann/Corbis, 31, 50, 52, 78, 84; William England/London Stereoscopic Company/Getty Images, 34; MPI/Getty Images, 36, 60, 82, 89, 90, 100 (top right), 101 (top); Rischgitz/Getty Images, 40; Three Lions/Getty Images, 47; The Granger Collection, New York, 48; Library of Congress, 58, 74, 100 (bottom right), 101 (bottom); Wesleyan University Library, Special Collections & Archives, 67; Library of Congress/Getty Images, 70, 100 (top left); The Schlesinger Library, Radcliffe Institute, Harvard University, 73; Samuel N. Fox/George Eastman House/Getty Images, 77; Photodisc, 96 (bottom); Evans/Three Lions/Getty Images, 98 (bottom); Texas State Library & Archives Commission, 100 (bottom).

31241008067806

Friendship According to Humphrey

Friendship According to Humphrey

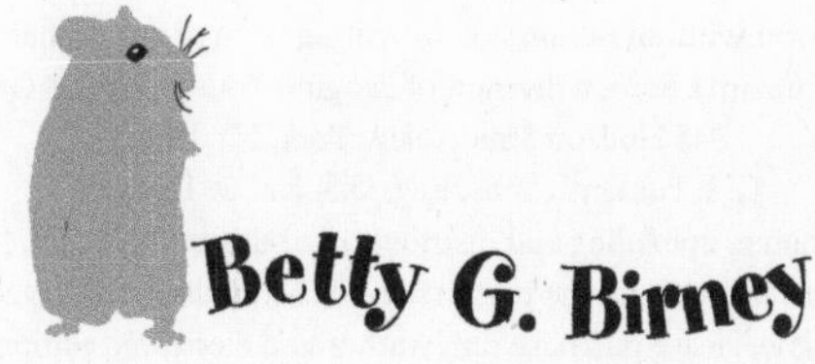

Betty G. Birney

G. P. Putnam's Sons • New York

G.P. PUTNAM'S SONS
A division of Penguin Young Readers Group
Published by The Penguin Group
Penguin Group (USA) Inc., 375 Hudson Street, New York, NY 10014, U.S.A.
Penguin Group (Canada), 10 Alcorn Avenue, Toronto, Ontario, Canada M4V 3B2
(a division of Pearson Penguin Canada Inc.)
Penguin Books Ltd, 80 Strand, London WC2R 0RL, England.
Penguin Ireland, 25 St. Stephen's Green, Dublin 2, Ireland
(a division of Penguin Books Ltd.)
Penguin Books India Pvt Ltd, 11 Community Centre, Panchsheel Park,
New Delhi - 110 017, India.
Penguin Group (NZ), Cnr Airborne and Rosedale Roads, Albany, Auckland,
New Zealand (a division of Pearson New Zealand Ltd).
Penguin Books (South Africa) (Pty) Ltd, 24 Sturdee Avenue, Rosebank,
Johannesburg 2196, South Africa.
Penguin Books Ltd, Registered Offices: 80 Strand, London WC2R 0RL, England.

Published simultaneously in Canada. Printed in the United States of America.
Designed by Gina DiMassi. Text set in Stempel Schneidler.

Library of Congress Cataloging-in-Publication Data
Birney, Betty G. Friendship according to Humphrey / Betty G. Birney. p. cm.
Sequel to: The world according to Humphrey. Summary: When Humphrey the hamster returns
to Mrs. Brisbane's class after the winter break, a new class pet and some other surprises
give him an opportunity to reflect on the meaning of friendship.
[1. Hamsters—Fiction. 2. Frogs—Fiction. 3. Schools—Fiction. 4. Friendship—Fiction.]
I. Title. PZ7.B52285Fr 2005 [Fic]—dc22 2004009538
ISBN 0-399-24264-3
9 10 8

To Jane Birney de Leeuw,
sister and friend,
and to Humphrey's BEST-BEST-BEST friend
and editor, Susan Kochan

Contents

Strange Change

BUMP-BUMP-BUMP!

Mrs. Brisbane and I were headed back to Longfellow School after the long winter holiday. But there were a lot more bumps in the road since the last time I rode in her small blue station wagon.

"Now, Humphrey," Mrs. Brisbane said. She was interrupted by another BUMP! "Don't be surprised." BUMP! "If there are a few changes." BUMP! "In Room Twenty-six." BUMP!

My stomach felt slightly queasy as I hung on tightly to my ladder, so I had a hard time understanding what she was telling me. What did she mean by "changes"?

"While you were home with Bert." BUMP! "I came back to school to get things all set."

I was home with her husband, Bert, a lot over the holidays, and as much as I like him, I was worn-out from running mazes a couple of times a day. Mr. Brisbane loves to watch me run mazes. At least back in school, I could catch forty winks once in a while. And since I am a classroom hamster, I belong in the classroom.

My stomach calmed down a bit as Mrs. Brisbane pulled her car into a parking space.

"Now, what about these changes?" I asked, but it came out as "Squeak-squeak-squeak," as usual.

"It's good to shake things up once in a while, Humphrey," Mrs. Brisbane assured me as she opened the car door. "You'll see."

I was already shaken up from the bumpy ride. Then a blast of icy wind made me shiver and I couldn't see a thing because Mrs. Brisbane had thrown a wool scarf over my cage. I didn't mind, as long as I was on the way back to my classroom, where I'd see all my friends again. Just thinking about them gave me a warm feeling. Or maybe it was the heat from the school furnace as we walked in the front door.

"Hi, Sue! Are we on for today?" a familiar voice called out. I couldn't see Miss Loomis, but I recognized her voice. Miss Loomis taught a class down the hall. She was also Mrs. Brisbane's friend.

"Sure, Angie. How about after morning recess?"

"See you then," said Miss Loomis.

Finally, Mrs. Brisbane set my cage down in Room 26 and removed the scarf. When she did, I was in for a shock. Something unsqueakable had happened to my classroom! For one thing, the tables faced the wrong direction. They used to point toward the front of the room. Now they were sideways.

Instead of being arranged in neat rows like before, the tables were clumped together in groups. Mrs. Brisbane's desk had moved to the corner of the room. Pictures of people I'd never seen before replaced the happy snowmen that had covered the bulletin board in December.

I was so dizzy from all the changes, I didn't notice the room filling up until Lower-Your-Voice-A.J. yelled, "Hiya, Humphrey!" as he came out of the cloakroom.

Soon, my other friends stopped by to say hello.

"Did you have a good vacation?" asked Miranda Golden. Miranda is an almost perfect human. That's why I think of her as Golden-Miranda.

"My mother says to tell you hi," Speak-Up-Sayeh said in her sweet, soft voice.

"Hey, Humphrey-Dumpty," Garth shouted. That made Gail snicker, but I didn't mind. She laughed at everything.

At that moment, the bell rang. "Class, look for your names and please take your seats now," Mrs. Brisbane said.

There was a lot of thumping and bumping as my classmates located their new seats. Now I had a better view of some of the students who used to sit on the opposite side of the room, like Don't-Complain-Mandy Payne, Sit-Still-Seth Stevenson and I-Heard-That-Kirk Chen. Maybe it is good to shake things up once in a while.

Then I noticed something odd. There was a stranger in Room 26, sitting near Sayeh, Gail and Kirk.

"Mrs. Brisbane, she doesn't belong here!" I squeaked out loud. "She's in the wrong room!"

Maybe Mrs. Brisbane didn't hear me.

"Class, as you can see, we're making some changes this year. And one of our changes is our brand-new pupil," the teacher announced. "Come here, Tabitha."

The new girl seemed SCARED-SCARED-SCARED as she got up and stood next to Mrs. Brisbane. "This is Tabitha Clark and I want you all to welcome her. Tabitha, why don't you tell us something about yourself?" The new girl looked down and shook her head. Mrs. Brisbane quickly turned back to the class. "We'll do that later. Now, who would like to be in charge of showing Tabitha around today?"

"Me!" a voice called out. Of course, it was Raise-Your-Hand-Heidi Hopper, who always forgets to raise her hand.

"Hands, please, Heidi. I think Mandy had her hand up first. Mandy, you will be Tabitha's buddy. I expect each of you to introduce yourself to Tabitha and include her in your activities." She turned to the girl. "I know you'll make a lot of good friends in Room Twenty-six. You may sit down now."

The girl kept staring down at the floor as she returned to her seat. She looked as if she needed a friend. I was so busy watching her, I only half listened to what Mrs. Brisbane was saying. Was she really talking about "poultry"?

"After all, this is Longfellow School," she said. "And as I hope you know, Henry Wadsworth Longfellow was a famous American poet."

Poetry! Nothing to do with chickens or turkeys, thank goodness. I have to admit, I'm a little scared of things with feathers, ever since my early days at Pet-O-Rama. I still have nightmares about the day a large green parrot escaped and flung himself at my cage, screeching, "Yum, yum! Time to eat! Bawk!" He was still shrieking as Carl, the store clerk, carried him away.

That unpleasant memory was interrupted when someone blurted, "I'm a poet and I don't know it. My feet show it—they're *long fellows*."

"I-Heard-That-Kirk," said Mrs. Brisbane. "Now, as I was saying, much of this term will be spent reading and writing poetry."

The groans were loud. I guess some people are afraid of poetry, even without feathers.

Seth squirmed in his seat and pretended to pound his head on the table. "Poetry," he moaned.

"Sit-Still-Seth," said Mrs. Brisbane.

Sitting still wasn't easy for Seth. Now that he was practically right in front of me, I could see him wiggling and jiggling in his chair, which made Gail Morgenstern laugh.

"Stop-Giggling-Gail!" Mrs. Brisbane warned.

Gail stopped giggling and started hiccuping.

"Please, go get a drink of water," Mrs. Brisbane told her. She turned to the new girl. "Tabitha, please put that toy away."

Everybody stared at Tabitha, including me. She was cradling a scruffy stuffed bear in her arms. The gray bear had cotton coming out of his ears and wore washed-out blue overalls with a button missing. Even his smile seemed a little faded.

"Now, please," said Mrs. Brisbane.

It was quiet in the room, thank goodness. I'm afraid if Gail had been there, we would have heard peals of laughter and heaps of hiccups!

Tabitha slid the shabby bear into the slot in her table without a word.

Right about then, Principal Morales marched through the door.

"Sorry for interrupting, Mrs. Brisbane. I just want to personally welcome you all back to school!"

The principal looked spiffy with a tie that had little pencils all over it. He always wore a tie because he was the Most Important Person at Longfellow School.

"Thank you, Mr. Morales," said Mrs. Brisbane. "We have a new student, Tabitha Clark, and a whole new setup for our class, as you can see."

"Welcome, Tabitha," said the principal. "I'm sure you'll love it here in Room Twenty-six. I'm glad to see that our friend Humphrey is back as well."

He walked all the way across the classroom to my cage.

"GLAD TO SEE YOU!" I squeaked in my loudest squeak.

"Hi, old pal," he greeted me. He turned back to the rest of the class. "You can all learn a lot from Humphrey. And I wish you a very successful semester."

After he left, I turned my attention back to Tabitha. She was still staring straight down. I couldn't see her face clearly, but it was almost as red as her copper-colored hair. I guess I watched her a long time, because suddenly, the recess bell rang.

"Come on, Tabitha, let's get our coats," Mandy said. Tabitha slipped the stuffed bear into her pocket and followed Mandy to the cloakroom.

As soon as the students were gone, Miss Loomis bustled into the room. Two pink dots of excitement colored her cheeks and her curls bounced in all directions.

"Are you ready? Should we do it?" she asked Mrs. Brisbane excitedly.

"Why not?" my teacher answered. "I'll make room for him now."

They walked over to the table in front of the window where my cage sits.

"Sure, he'll fit right here," said Miss Loomis, pointing to a spot near my house.

Mrs. Brisbane slid some of my supplies down to the end of the table. "Now, you're sure he's not a lot of trouble?"

"Oh, no. Not nearly as much trouble as a hamster," Miss Loomis answered.

WHAT-WHAT-WHAT? Not nearly as much trouble as a hamster! Since when have I caused any trouble in Room 26? Since when did I not totally dedicate myself to helping my classmates and teacher? Surprisingly, Mrs. Brisbane didn't correct her. I was about to squeak up for myself when the bell rang again and Miss Loomis scurried out of the room.

I wondered *who* wasn't as much trouble as I am. "He," Miss Loomis had said.

He who? Curiosity made my whiskers twitch and my paws tingle.

My fur was practically standing on end as the tables filled up. I saw Tabitha slip her bear out of her pocket. Heidi saw it, too, and rolled her eyes at Gail, who almost giggled but managed to stop herself.

"Now, class, I told you there were some changes in our room this year," Mrs. Brisbane announced. "Another of the changes is a brand-new classroom pet. I think he'll add a lot to Room Twenty-six."

New classroom pet? Why did she want a new classroom pet when she already had a wonderful, terrific—okay, perfect—classroom pet, namely me? Was I being replaced?

Miss Loomis entered, carrying a large glass tank. I couldn't see what it was because my classmates were standing up, craning their necks, *ooh*-ing and *ahh*-ing, and chattering away.

"It's a frog!" shouted Heidi.

Miss Loomis set the glass box right next to my cage. Now I could see some water, rocks, and something green and REALLY-REALLY-REALLY lumpy.

"Meet our new frog," said Mrs. Brisbane. "Miss Loomis will tell you about him."

"Well, boys and girls, as you may know, we have a

frog in our classroom. His name is George and he's a bullfrog. Right before the holidays, one of our students brought in this frog to keep George company. We named him Og the Frog. Unfortunately, George didn't like Og. And being a bullfrog, George let us know he didn't like Og by making a *lot* of noise. That upset Og, I guess, because he would leap and splash all day long while George was croaking."

My classmates laughed, but I didn't. On the one paw, I could see why George didn't want another frog to compete with. On the other paw, croaking at Og wasn't a very friendly way to act.

"With all the noise, we were having trouble getting any work done at all," Miss Loomis continued. "So I asked Mrs. Brisbane if your class would like to have Og, and she said yes. He's a very quiet frog. Do you like him?"

My friends all yelled, "YES!" Everyone except Tabitha, who was secretly petting her little bear.

Somebody went "Ribbit-ribbit" in a funny croaking voice. It wasn't the frog.

"I-Heard-That-Kirk. That's quite enough. Og can provide the sound effects from now on. I think he'll make a nice friend for Humphrey," Mrs. Brisbane said.

A friend for me? At least he wasn't my replacement—whew! But I was already friends with every single person in Room 26, so she didn't really need to find me another one. Still, I didn't want to act unfriendly, the way George had.

After Miss Loomis left, Mrs. Brisbane let the students have a closer look at Og.

Seth tapped at the glass.

"Don't do that, Seth," the teacher warned him. "You'll frighten him."

"He doesn't seem frightened of anything," Miranda observed.

"I think he's smiling," added Kirk. "That must mean he's *hoppy*."

For once, Gail didn't giggle, which seemed to bother Kirk. "Get it? Hoppy? Happy?" he tried to explain.

Gail rolled her eyes and groaned, which didn't make Kirk hoppy at all.

Mrs. Brisbane called to the new girl. "Come see Og, Tabitha."

Tabitha stared down at her table and shook her head no.

"Come on, Tabitha!" Mandy sounded impatient.

Again, Tabitha shook her head.

"She hasn't wanted to do anything all day!" Mandy grumbled.

"Mandy . . . ," Mrs. Brisbane warned her.

"Is he really a frog?" Richie stared hard at Og, who stared right back. "Don't frogs live in water?"

"Some do," said Mrs. Brisbane. "And some frogs live in trees. Og is a common green frog. He likes to live near the water, but not in it. That's why he has a tank that's half land and half water."

A common green frog didn't sound very interesting,

but Og had certainly attracted the attention of my classmates.

"Can I take care of Og?" A.J. asked loudly.

"Lower-Your-Voice-A.J.," said Mrs. Brisbane. "We will all take care of him."

Once the students returned to their seats, Mrs. Brisbane held up a book on the care of frogs. "We'll have to study this," she explained. "Taking care of Og will be quite different from caring for Humphrey. After all, Humphrey is a warm-blooded mammal. Og is a cold-blooded amphibian."

Amphibian! That's nothing like a mammal. The very word made my warm blood run cold! I hoped that she would never, ever put that word on a spelling test.

Mrs. Brisbane looked through the book. "Aha," she said. "It says that the common green frog is a medium-sized frog with a calm nature. It makes a distinctive twanging sound."

"BOING!"

I almost fell off my ladder. What on earth could that noise be?

Then I heard another sound: the laughter of my classmates.

"That certainly is a distinctive twanging sound," said Mrs. Brisbane, looking puzzled.

"BOING!" This time, the noise was clearly coming from the frog. What kind of way is that to talk? Aren't frogs supposed to say "Ribbit"?

Mrs. Brisbane turned toward Og's glass box. "Thank you for the demonstration, Og."

Then I heard: "Boing-boing-boing!" It didn't come from the frog this time.

"I-Heard-That-Kirk Chen," said the teacher. She continued to talk on and on about amphibians and their life cycle.

"What does he eat?" Heidi called out.

"Hands, please, Heidi," said Mrs. Brisbane wearily. "Mostly insects. Miss Loomis gave me a container of crickets."

"Cool!" said Kirk.

Everybody else in the class groaned. "Ewwwww!"

When I finished gagging, I squeaked, "LIVE insects?" Not that anyone was listening to me. Especially not Og, who calmly sat there doing absolutely nothing.

At the end of the day, as the students gathered up their books and coats and filed past our table, at least half of them said, "Bye, Og," or "Catch you later, Oggy."

Not one of my classmates said good-bye to me. I guess they all forgot.

Mandy stayed for a minute after class. "Mrs. Brisbane, you told me to be friendly to that new girl, but she isn't very friendly back."

"Don't-Complain-Mandy," said the teacher. "It's not easy to be the new kid in the classroom. Put yourself in her shoes. Give her some time. After all, we've got the whole semester ahead of us."

A whole semester ahead of us—and I had to spend it with a frog?

Mrs. Brisbane had shaken things up all right. And I felt queasy all over again.

"The better part of one's life consists of his friendships."

Abraham Lincoln, sixteenth president of the United States

Upset Pet

I'd had bad days before. The worst day was when Ms. Mac left. She was the substitute teacher who found me at Pet-O-Rama and brought me to Room 26. She almost broke my heart by moving to Brazil, which is so far away.

I'd also overcome problems before. Like getting Mrs. Brisbane and her husband, Bert, to go from not liking me to liking me a WHOLE-WHOLE-WHOLE lot.

But I'd never had a problem like this: how to make friends with a frog. Back in my early days at Pet-O-Rama, I'd met guinea pigs, mice, rats, gerbils and chinchillas in the Small Pet Department. If there were frogs around, they must have been over with the fish and less interesting pets.

After school was over, Mrs. Brisbane gathered up her coat, gloves and books, walked over to Og and me and said, "Well, fellows, you're on your own tonight. Have fun!"

And with that, she left.

I recalled the first night I was alone in Room 26. As it slowly got dark outside, I slowly got scared inside. I would have liked a friend to talk to that night. Maybe Og felt the same way. Like Tabitha, Og was new to the class, and I thought I should try and make friends with him. Mrs. Brisbane had said it's not easy to be new. You should always listen to your teacher.

"Don't worry, Og," I squeaked to him. "They'll all be back tomorrow. And Aldo will be here later."

I waited for an answer. All I heard was silence. I knew he probably couldn't understand me. Still, I'd learned to understand what humans said, and for the most part, they seemed to understand me when I chose to squeak up. Surely I could do as well with a frog. I decided to try again.

"CAN YOU HEAR ME?" I squeaked as loudly as possible.

Either he couldn't hear me or he was just plain rude. I couldn't see him all that well from my cage, what with my wheel, my ladders, tree branches, sleeping house and mirror. Since I knew Aldo wouldn't come in to clean the room for hours, I decided to introduce myself. As an experienced (and well-loved) classroom pet, I could share my wealth of knowledge about the schedule, the students and the studies in Room 26. Og could come to me for advice whenever he wanted.

After all, you can learn a lot by taking care of another species, as Ms. Mac told me. Surely that included frogs.

I easily opened the door to my cage. It has a lock-that-doesn't-lock. However, I'm the only one who knows about it. To humans, it looks like it's tightly latched, but trust me, it's not.

"I'm coming over, Og," I announced.

Again, there was no response. I scampered over to meet my new roommate anyway.

The glass tank had a big dish of water on one side and pebbles and plants on the other. There was a screen over the top. Sitting under a large green plant was a large green lump.

I tiptoed over close to the glass and peered in.

The lump was even uglier than I first thought. At least compared to me. After all, I am a Golden Hamster with soft fur, dark, inquisitive eyes and a little pink nose. Intelligent humans such as Miranda Golden and Sayeh Nasiri have told me I am cute.

This Og-thing, on the other hand, was a sickening shade of green with bulging eyes and not a bit of fur on him. Even worse, he had a huge mouth—as wide as his whole body—that curved up at the ends as if he were grinning. He didn't look happy, just creepy. I tried not to shudder.

"Allow me to introduce myself. I am your neighbor, Humphrey," I squeaked as politely as possible.

No answer. Maybe he couldn't hear me. After all, he didn't have cute rounded ears like me. He didn't seem to have ears at all. But at least he could see I was acting in a friendly manner.

"OG?" Stepping closer, I squeaked a bit louder this

time. "Even though we don't know each other, I'm happy to extend the paw of friendship—"

Then, with no warning at all, Og lunged right at me and let out a very loud "Boing!"

I must have leaped a foot backward! Og couldn't get through the glass, but goodness, he startled me!

"I was only trying to be friendly," I told him, backing up toward my cage.

"Boing!" He sounded like a broken guitar string.

I sneaked a peek at him. Was that grin a leer? Or a sneer?

My heart was still pounding as I darted back into my cage and slammed the door behind me. Some friend Og was, scaring me like that!

I tried to put myself in his shoes, like Mrs. Brisbane said, but he didn't wear any. Neither did I, for that matter.

I grabbed the tiny notebook and pencil from behind my mirror. Ms. Mac gave them to me. No one in Room 26 knew about them. No one knew I could read and write. Writing helps me sort out my thoughts. And I had a lot of thoughts rolling around my brain that night—not all of them nice.

I scribbled away for several hours and Og was pretty quiet, except for some annoying splashing. Goodness, I can manage to groom myself and get a drink of water without making that much noise!

Suddenly, the room filled with blazing light and I

heard a familiar CLANG-CLANG-CLANG. It was the Longfellow School custodian, Aldo Amato.

"Be of good cheer 'cause Aldo's here!" a voice announced.

"Aldo! My friend!" I squeaked as I jumped on my wheel and began spinning happily.

Aldo parked his cleaning cart near the door and clumped over to my cage.

"Happy New Year, Humphrey! You're looking handsome and healthy," he told me.

Aldo is a true friend!

"And you, the same," I squeaked back.

"Who's your buddy?" Aldo glanced at Og. "Hey, I know you. The frog from down the hall. What are you doing here?"

"You don't want to know!" I squeaked.

Aldo turned back to me. "Calm down, pal, I brought you something." He reached into his pocket and unwrapped the most beautiful tiny tomato I've ever seen. I could have cried.

"Thanks, Aldo," I squeaked as I tucked the treat in my cheek pouch.

"You're welcome, Humphrey." Aldo looked over at Og again. "Sorry, I don't know what frogs eat."

"You don't want to know that, either!" I assured him.

Aldo grabbed a paper bag and pulled a chair up close to me. "May I join you for dinner?" he asked.

He didn't need to ask. We'd shared many happy evenings while he took his dinner break. I took a deep breath. Aldo gave off a pleasant smell of chalk dust and pine spray. He smelled the way I imagined a forest smells. Somewhere, WAY-WAY-WAY back in time, wild hamsters must have lived in forests, down in sweet earthy piles of rotting leaves and fallen pinecones. Yep, Aldo smelled like home!

"Mind if we have a little talk?" he asked.

Of course I didn't. I'd been trying to get old lumpy to talk all evening.

"I got something to tell you, Humph. Remember how I gave my girlfriend, Maria, an engagement ring for Christmas? Well, I've got bigger news. On New Year's Day, she and I ran off and got married!" He held up his left hand. A gold band glittered on one finger.

"I hope you'll be HAPPY-HAPPY-HAPPY!" I squeaked with delight.

"Thanks, pal. I know I told you that you'd be at my wedding, but we decided to get hitched quietly. You understand?" he asked.

Naturally I squeaked, "Yes." After all, I'd helped them get together in the first place. And when I met Maria, she was as nice as Aldo.

"Yep, I'm an old married man now. Real happy. But I've started thinking, Humphrey. I like this job, but it doesn't pay a whole lot." Aldo paused to chew a bite of his sandwich. "I'd like to have kids and a house and maybe raise a couple of hamsters of my own."

Fine with me, as long as he didn't raise any frogs.

"I sure would love to have my evenings free to spend

with my family. Pal, I've got to find a way to get a better job," Aldo continued.

"You can do it!" I squeaked.

Aldo was quieter than usual as he finished his dinner. I spun on my wheel to entertain him, but he was lost in thought. Finally, he folded up his bag.

"Guess I'm not good company tonight, Humphrey. I bet that frog makes better conversation than I do."

"Fat chance," I squeaked.

After Aldo cleaned the room and left, I did some thinking. Personally, I believed Aldo was already as fine a human as I've ever seen. I'd miss him if he worked somewhere else. But he was my friend, so if he wanted a better job, I wanted to help him.

I started jotting down ideas in my notebook and lost track of time. Later, I heard splashing. I'd almost forgotten about you-know-who next door.

"Hey, what's shaking, Og?" I called out to him. Maybe he'd thought over his bad behavior and wanted to apologize for his bad manners.

There was no reply, just splish-splash-splish. Personally, the idea of being covered in water is disgusting to me. I prefer to groom myself the time-honored way: using the tongue, teeth, paws and toenails. I thoroughly clean myself every day. The students in Room 26 love to watch me. At least they did before google-eyes came along.

Still, if I had to share a table with him, I figured I

might TRY-TRY-TRY again to be friendly. "Having a nice bath?" I asked.

There was no answer. Not even another splash. But there was another sound: the crickets. So they were alive after all!

Og *would* have to eat noisy food. My Nutri-Nibbles and Mighty Mealworms didn't make a sound until I crunched down on them. But the crickets—whom I actually felt sorry for—made a funny singing song: "Chirrup, chirrup!" Apparently, they were nocturnal, like me.

It was going to be a long night with noisy crickets and a silent frog. I hopped on my wheel and tried to spin my irritation away.

It didn't work.

"The only way to have a friend is to be one."

Ralph Waldo Emerson, American poet and essayist

Sad-Mad-Bad

I'll tell you how the whole week went: TERRIBLE-TERRIBLE-TERRIBLE! It must have been National Frog Appreciation Week, because frogs were all we talked about in Room 26.

First, Mrs. Brisbane taught everybody how to take care of Og. The students gathered around as she put on rubber gloves, picked up the insect container and sprinkled a few into Og's tank. She didn't seem too happy about the crickets, which turned out to be quite large and ugly. The way they leaped around the tank, no wonder Og went "Boing!"

"Did you see his tongue?" A.J. bellowed. "It must be a foot long!"

"Oooh, he ate one!" Heidi squealed.

"Gross!" said Seth as Og's tongue grabbed the rest of the crickets.

"I want to pet him," said Mandy. Before anyone could stop her, she slid the top off the tank, reached down and picked up the big lump of frog.

"No, Mandy!" said Mrs. Brisbane. But it was too late.

"He peed on me!" Mandy shrieked, dropping Og back into his tank. Not that I blamed her. What unsqueakably bad manners! Is that any way for a classroom pet to act?

Seth jumped back, shaking his hands. "Oooh!"

Gail giggled, of course, as did everyone else.

"Wash your hands with plenty of soap and hot water," Mrs. Brisbane told Mandy. To the rest of the class, she said, "That's what frogs do when they're frightened. We must all be gentle with poor Og. If you have to touch him, you must wear gloves. Pick him up by the shoulder blades and never squeeze his stomach or you'll hurt him."

She ordered my classmates back to their seats (not including Mandy, who was washing her hands). Then we had to learn more frog facts. They don't start out as cute, furry little babies like hamsters. NO-NO-NO! They start out as funny little tadpoles, then grow into ugly-looking pollywogs and end up as big, lumpy frogs with bulgy eyes.

For some strange reason, everyone was fascinated with frogs, except Tabitha and me. She paid more attention to her stuffed bear than to anything else in class.

I overheard Mandy complain to the other girls that Tabitha wasn't very friendly. "I tried to get her to play at recess, but she wasn't interested in anything besides that old bear. She's a big baby."

Sayeh murmured, "Maybe she's shy." I was pleased

that Sayeh had learned to speak up. But the other girls decided Tabitha was just unfriendly.

Like someone else who was new to Room 26.

After so much frog talk, Mrs. Brisbane moved on to the subject of poetry.

First, we read a scary poem about a tiger. We also read a poem about a bee, followed by a silly poem about a purple cow. Some poems rhyme and some don't. But there are a lot of rhyming words, like "moon" and "June," and "cat" and "rat." (Funny that those last two words rhyme, isn't it?)

At night, while Og stared into space, I made lists of rhyming words in my notebook. Better than trying to talk to him, as he continued to give me the silent treatment.

Jumpy, bumpy, grumpy, lumpy. Funny that those words rhyme, too!

After a few days spent reading poems, Mrs. Brisbane said it was time for us to write our own poems. There were louder groans than the first time she mentioned poetry. Mrs. Brisbane held up her hand, which meant everybody had to be quiet.

"All of this is in preparation for Valentine's Day, when our class will present a Poetry Festival for all the parents. Each of you will recite a poem you wrote or one you like." There were no groans now. In fact, some of the students looked excited. Even Pay-Attention-Art Patel was paying attention.

Mrs. Brisbane explained that our assignment was to

write a poem about an animal, at least six lines long, with words that rhymed.

Mandy raised her hand and the teacher called on her. "My name rhymes with 'candy cane,' " she proudly announced.

Mrs. Brisbane smiled. "That's right. 'Mandy Payne' rhymes with 'candy cane.' Does anyone else have a rhyming name?"

" 'Richie' rhymes with 'itchy'!" A.J. blurted out.

"What?" asked Repeat-It-Please-Richie.

Words were flying through my brain. Humphrey-pumphrey-dumphrey-lumphrey.

" 'Gail' rhymes with 'hail'!" Heidi forgot to raise her hand again.

"And 'fail,' " Kirk muttered.

"I-Heard-That-Kirk Chen," said Mrs. Brisbane.

"Well, 'Kirk' rhymes with 'jerk,' " said Heidi, who was always ready to defend her best friend, Gail.

"Please, no more," Mrs. Brisbane said firmly. " 'Kirk' also rhymes with 'work.' So let's get back to work."

I never saw my classmates work so hard before. Richie chewed on his pencil, Seth jiggled his leg, Heidi erased more than she wrote, Kirk scratched his head and Miranda wrote and wrote and wrote. Then she stopped writing and raised her hand.

"Mrs. Brisbane, can you think of anything that rhymes with 'hamster'?" she asked.

"Let's throw that one out to the class," said the teacher. "Anyone?"

Leave it to Golden-Miranda to ask such a good question. It got everybody thinking, because it was so quiet, you could have heard a pencil drop. Two pencils did drop, in fact.

"How about 'gangster'?" a voice called out.

"Raise-Your-Hand-Heidi." Mrs. Brisbane walked to the board. "How about that, class? Does 'HAMster' rhyme with 'GANGster'?"

She wrote the words on the board and repeated them. "Hear that? They don't have quite the same sound, do they?"

Well, I would hope not! Gangsters are bad guys and I am definitely a good guy.

"Maybe you'd better find another word to rhyme," the teacher instructed.

"Try 'Humphrey'!" I squeaked in encouragement. There had to be something that rhymed.

"Try 'frog'!" shouted A.J.

"Lower-Your-Voice-A.J.," Mrs. Brisbane reminded him.

"And raise your hand," added Heidi.

Mrs. Brisbane shook her head, then began to write words on the board as my classmates shouted them out. Dog, fog, log, slog, clog and more.

Nothing rhymed with "hamster," but everything rhymed with "frog." How depressing! I wondered how many words rhyme with "sad"? Like "mad" and "bad."

After recess, it was Miranda's turn to clean my cage. She always does an extra-good job of cleaning my potty corner and changing my water and bedding. And she always has a special treat for me, like a piece of cauliflower. Yum.

"Sorry, Humphrey. I tried to write a poem about you," she told me. "I think I'm going to have to write about Clem instead."

Clem was Miranda's dog, the one who tried to eat me when I stayed at her house. How Golden-Miranda could put up with Clem was beyond me.

That night, I wrote my very first poem ever. I asked Og if he wanted to hear it. His silence wasn't too encouraging, but I decided to read it anyway.

When Ms. Mac left me for Brazil,
She made me SAD-SAD-SAD.

When Clem the dog was mean to me,
I felt real MAD-MAD-MAD.

Now Og's moved in and he has got me
Feeling BAD-BAD-BAD.

In fact, this is the worst week
I ever HAD-HAD-HAD!

I waited to hear Og applaud or at least give me a grudging "Boing." I heard only silence. When I glanced over at my neighbor, he was grinning from ear to ear. Or he would have been if he had ears. Somehow, his smile didn't cheer me up at all.

I felt better the following day, though, because it was Friday. That meant I would get a little break from Room 26 and the green and grumpy lump. Every weekend, a different student took me home, and I'd had many wonderful adventures with my classmates and their families. I'd even gone home with Principal Morales!

This week, I was going home with Wait-For-The-Bell-Garth Tugwell. He'd wanted to take me home for a long time.

"Can I take Og home, too?" asked Garth.

"I think Og can stay here," Mrs. Brisbane answered. "Frogs don't need to eat every day, except when they're young."

Funny, I didn't feel quite so sad-mad-bad anymore.

"Can't your mom pick us up?" A.J. asked Garth after school.

I couldn't see him, but I could hear him as we waited outside for the bus. I had a blanket over my cage because it was cold outside. I didn't mind, though, as long as I was FAR-FAR-FAR away from Og. (Who hadn't even tried to say "good-bye" to me.)

"My dad said not to bother her. She's been sick," said Garth. "Couldn't your mom pick us up?"

"I wish." A.J. sighed. "She has to pick up my sister from kindergarten and put the baby down for a nap."

"Did you tell your folks about Bean?" asked Garth.

At least I thought he said "Bean." Things sounded a little muffled under the blanket.

"Naw," said A.J. "Last time I said somebody was picking on me, my dad signed me up for boxing lessons. I hated people punching me. It was worse than being picked on."

I tried to sort out what A.J. meant about getting picked on. By a bean? By a boxing bean? I didn't have time to figure it out before the bus arrived.

"Here goes," said Garth, lifting my cage. "Let's stick together, no matter what."

"Okay. Be sure to sit in front by Miss Victoria," whispered A.J. "That's the safest."

By the shuffling and scuffling sounds, I could tell that we were on the bus. Luckily, a corner of the blanket slipped down and I could see Miss Victoria, the bus driver, glancing over her shoulder.

"Keep moving, guys," she said in a firm voice. "Whoa, ladies, one of you has to go. Can't have three in a seat." Three first-grade girls were huddled together in the seat right behind the bus driver. "We're not moving until one of you goes. You move, Beth."

The girl on the end timidly got up and started down the aisle, nervously looking back at her friends.

"Keep going, folks," Miss Victoria snapped.

Suddenly—BOOM! The girl named Beth fell down flat on the floor right in front of us. Her books slid around the floor in all directions.

The bus was quiet as Beth lay there until somebody said, "Hey, klutz, you dropped something!" That was followed by a nasty snicker.

"You tripped her," said A.J. in a voice not quite as loud as usual.

"Says you, A.J.! What do those letters stand for, anyway? Awful Jerk?"

I crawled over to the side of the cage to see who was speaking. He was BIG-BIG-BIG for a kid. He had spiky hair and a scowl on his face.

As Garth and A.J. bent over to help Beth pick up her books, Miss Victoria called to the back of the bus.

"Garth and A.J., if you don't sit down so I can get moving, I'm going to report you two."

"Yeah, Garth Bugwart, sit down," the big kid sneered.

"I'm going to tell," Beth said softly.

"Don't!" A.J. whispered back. "Bean will only get worse."

So this was the scary Bean they were talking about!

Beth slid into a seat with all her books. Just as A.J. stepped forward, Bean stuck his leg into the aisle. So that's how he had tripped her! After A.J. managed to step over it, Garth and I (in my cage) were standing right next to Mr. Nasty.

"What's in the cage, Bugface? Your lunch?" He snorted a few times, but no one else on the bus laughed. "Or is that your girlfriend?"

That did it! I was fighting mad. Somebody had to squeak up to this guy. "For your information, I am a male Golden Hamster. And you are one MEAN BEAN!"

"Anybody got a mousetrap?" Bean snarled.

"Why aren't you guys in your seats?" Miss Victoria

yelled from the front of the bus. "I'm writing you up, Garth and A.J.!"

Garth slid into a seat next to A.J. I was about to give Miss Victoria a piece of my mind when the bus lurched forward and I had to hold on to my cage for dear life. I was sorry I'd eaten those Nutri-Nibbles just before we left.

All week, I'd been looking forward to going home with Garth. Now, I wasn't sure I'd ever make it there!

"Friendship is one mind in two bodies."

Mencius, Chinese philosopher

Mean Bean

A.J.'s stop was before Garth's. "Come on over tomorrow," Garth told his friend. As soon as A.J. left, Garth moved up to the front of the bus to get away from Bean.

"What part of 'sit down' don't you understand, Garth?" Miss Victoria sounded pretty irritated.

"Sorry. The cage wouldn't fit on the seat," he said.

"What on earth is in there, anyway?"

Before Garth could answer, the bus stopped in front of his house. He pulled the blanket down around my cage and hurried down the steps.

Mrs. Tugwell was waiting in the doorway of the house. She had wavy brown hair like her son. She had glasses and freckles like her son, too. She helped him set my cage up on the family room table. Garth's little brother, Andy, raced into the room. He had wavy brown hair, glasses and freckles, too. "Mine!" he shouted.

"Nope. He's mine. At least for the weekend," said Garth.

"Tell Andy about Humphrey," Garth's mom said.

"He's a hamster. And you have to be nice to him," Garth explained.

He got that right!

"I like ham," said Andy, rubbing his stomach. "Yum-yum!"

I hopped onto my wheel to show Andy that a hamster wasn't anything like a ham.

"Wheee! Ham go 'round!" said Andy.

Garth's mother brought in a plate of peanut butter and crackers. Ooh, that smelled good!

"How was school?" she asked.

"Okay," said Garth. "But Mom, could you say something to Bean's mom? He's mean to everybody on the bus."

"Martin Bean?" Garth's mom sounded surprised. "Why, he's always polite when I see him."

"Well, he's not polite any other time," Garth explained. "He tripped a girl on the bus and called everybody names."

"That doesn't sound like Martin. What did the bus driver do?"

"Nothing," Garth answered.

"Well, I think she should be the one to work things out," said Mrs. Tugwell.

"But you're friends with Mrs. Bean!"

"I probably won't be if I complain about her son. Maybe if you were friendlier to him, he'd act nicer."

"Mom . . . ," Garth moaned.

"It's worth a try," his mom suggested.

I had to squeak up. "He's the Meanest Bean I've ever seen!"

"Goodness, what's the matter with Humphrey?" asked Mrs. Tugwell.

"Maybe he doesn't like Marty, either," Garth muttered. He's one smart guy.

Shortly after Mr. Tugwell came home, Natalie arrived. She was the babysitter, but I didn't see any babies around for her to sit on. Garth wasn't a baby, Andy wasn't a baby and certainly I was no baby.

Natalie had black hair and wore a black shirt, black pants and black shoes. She had glasses with black frames. Her lips were bright red.

"Order a pizza," said Garth's dad, handing Natalie some money. "I got some videos for the guys."

"Okay," said Natalie. "Mind if I do some homework?"

"As long as you get the boys in bed at nine," Mrs. Tugwell explained.

Natalie glanced at my cage. "What about the rat?"

I felt quite discouraged. I'd already been called a mouse and a ham that day.

"He's a hammer!" Andy yelled.

"Oh, a hamster. How cute," said Natalie, leaning in toward my cage. "Hi there, big boy."

Whew! After a miserable week and a rough ride home, I suddenly felt a whole lot better.

Later, the boys ate pizza and watched videos while Natalie read from a big thick book.

"What's that?" asked Andy, leaning over her shoulder. "How come it doesn't have any pictures?"

"College books don't have pictures."

Andy wrinkled his nose. "What's college?"

Natalie sighed. "After you go to high school and graduate, if you want a good job like a doctor or a lawyer or a teacher, you have to go to college."

"I know that," Garth piped in. "City College is right down the street. Mom took classes there last year."

"That's where I go," said Natalie. "I'm studying psychology." The way she said it, that big word sounded like "sigh-coll-uh-gee." But the word on her book was spelled "Psychology." I wrote it down in my notebook later. (I hope that word is never on a spelling test!)

"In psychology, you find out what's inside people's heads." The babysitter reached for Andy's head.

"Ooey-gooey brains," said Garth.

"Don't go in my head!" screamed Andy, leaping off the couch.

Natalie laughed. "Not like that. Psychology teaches you how people think. Do you know what I'm thinking?"

Andy shook his head.

"I'm thinking it's time for bed," Natalie said. "Nine o'clock."

The boys both groaned. "Not yet," Garth protested.

Andy folded his arms. "You can't make me!" he said firmly.

Surprisingly, Natalie sat back and smiled. "I guess you're right. I can't make you."

Andy's eyes practically bugged out of his head. "Huh?"

"Why don't you put on another video? We can stay up till your parents get back," the babysitter continued. "It'll be fun!"

"Yes!" Garth exclaimed as he and his brother gleefully high-fived each other.

But I was a little confused. Hadn't Mrs. Tugwell told her to get the boys in bed at nine? I was sure that Natalie had lost her mind.

Garth settled back on the couch, but after a minute, his smile disappeared. "When do you think Mom and Dad will be back?"

Natalie shrugged her shoulders. "They didn't say."

"Won't they be upset if we're still up?"

"I guess we'll find out, won't we?" Natalie answered with a mischievous grin.

Andy looked worried. "They'll be mad if we're not in bed."

"So?" said Natalie. "We still have time to watch more TV."

Garth stood up and yawned loudly. "I'm kind of tired."

"Me, too," said Andy, stretching his arms.

Natalie smiled. "Well, if you really think so, okay. You two get ready for bed and I'll be up in a minute."

As the brothers raced upstairs, Natalie chuckled to herself, then leaned in toward my cage.

"And that, Humphrey Hamster, is what is called 'reverse psychology.' You get people to do what you want by telling them to do the opposite."

Reverse psychology. (Remember, it's pronounced sigh-coll-uh-gee.) So that's how people's minds work. Just tell them to do the opposite of what you want them to do.

You can sure learn a lot at college.

You can learn a lot from a good babysitter, too.

The next afternoon, A.J. came over to Garth's house to play. Mrs. Tugwell took Andy out to buy new shoes. Mr. Tugwell was paying bills in the kitchen. The boys were alone with me in the family room.

"Humphrey needs some exercise," said A.J. "Let's take him out."

"Okay. You can watch him while I clean his cage."

A.J. gently took me out while Garth put on gloves and began to clean my cage. Both boys chuckled when he got to my potty corner—everyone does—but he did a good job of cleaning it. While he worked, they talked.

"Any chance your dad can drive us Monday morning?" asked Garth.

A.J. shook his head as he gently petted me. "He has to leave for work real early. How about your dad?"

Garth shook his head. "He always talks about how he had to walk to school and how lucky I am to ride a bus."

"I know." A.J. sighed and set me down on the table.

"Watch it!" said Garth. He set a row of big tall books all around the edge of the table. "We don't want Humphrey to get away."

"Maybe he'll be sick on Monday," Garth suggested.

"Are you kidding? He's the healthiest guy at school. Man, if he wasn't so big, I'd really give it to him," said A.J., making a fist.

"Me, too," Garth agreed.

It wasn't hard to figure out that they were talking about big mean Marty Bean.

"I don't know why Miss Victoria always takes his side," Garth said after a while.

"He knows how not to get caught."

The boys were silent again until Garth said, "Miranda was getting a drink at the fountain at recess, and he came up and pushed her out of the way."

The thought of someone pushing Golden-Miranda, an almost perfect human, really ruffled my fur.

"Did she tell?" asked A.J.

"Yeah. He said he didn't do it," Garth explained. "Said he wasn't anywhere near her. He said Kirk did it. Kirk almost got in trouble, so Miranda said it was all a mistake to get Kirk off the hook."

"Kirk the Jerk. That's what Bean calls him," said Garth. "He's got a name for everybody. That's why he doesn't have any friends."

He stepped back and pulled off his rubber gloves. "I think that's one clean cage."

"Great," I squeaked. "But what are we going to do about Bean?"

"Bean's a pretty funny name," A.J. said with a chuckle. "Bean brain."

"Bean breath," said Garth.

The boys started laughing.

"Bean bag!"

"Bean jeans!"

"Green Bean!"

"Mean Bean! Hey—that rhymes! Mean green Bean!"

Mrs. Brisbane would be proud to hear them rhyming! I liked hearing them laugh. However, I was worried. Bean had said something about a mousetrap. The mere mention of those contraptions makes me shiver and quiver. And I didn't want to see anybody get tripped or pushed again.

"Ready to go back in, Humphrey-Dumpty?" asked Garth.

"YES!" I squeaked, which for some reason made the boys howl with laughter again.

Once I was back in the cage, the boys went up to play in Garth's room. That gave me time to think. Here were Garth and A.J., really good friends. They were nice to each other and stuck together. Marty Bean wasn't friendly to anybody and he didn't have any friends.

All my classmates liked Og, but when I offered to be his friend, he leaped at me in a very rude way. The business of friendship is not as easy as it sounds, I figured, just before dozing off for a long afternoon nap.

It was nice at Garth's house that weekend. The announcer on TV said it was COLD-COLD-COLD outside, so the Tugwells stayed inside. The family popped popcorn—did that smell good! And they watched TV and snuggled on the couch. As happy as I should have been, I worried about Monday's bus ride. What I needed was a Plan. And maybe a little psychology.

"Are you sure the little guy won't catch cold?" asked Mrs. Tugwell as Garth was ready to leave for school on Monday.

"He's got a fur coat. And I'll cover him," Garth assured her. I was plunged into total darkness as he threw a blanket over the cage.

"Bye, Ham!" shouted Andy.

"Bye, Andy!" I squeaked back. After all, a "ham" isn't the worst thing that a person can call you.

Soon, I heard the squeal of the bus's brakes as it stopped in front of the Tugwells' house.

"All aboard!" I heard Miss Victoria say. "Find a seat."

"This cage is too big. Can't I sit up here?" asked Garth.

"Do you see any empty seats up here?" the bus driver replied. "Get moving and keep moving."

I was already queasy just thinking about Bean. As Garth walked toward the back of the bus, looking for an empty seat, my cage swayed back and forth like a ship on a rough sea, which didn't help my stomach at all.

Once we sat down, the bus started rolling. A block later, it abruptly stopped and I slid across the floor of my cage. Ouch!

"All aboard!" I heard Miss Victoria say. "Find a seat, A.J."

A.J. walked back to our seat. "Move over," he told Garth.

"I have to sit on the aisle," Garth replied. "The cage won't fit in the seat."

A.J. crawled over Garth so he was close to the window. As he did, he bent down and whispered, "Told you he'd be here. He's always here."

As the bus lurched forward, my cage wobbled enough for the blanket to part, so I could see a little. And what I saw was most unpleasant: Marty Bean sitting right next to us.

"Hey, Garth, is that your face or did somebody throw up on you?" I could see the smirk on his face as he leaned in close, mere inches from my cage.

"Is that a cage, Bugwart, or is it your purse?" Bean asked. He hooted at his own joke even though it wasn't funny.

It may have been cold outside, but I was getting pretty hot. Og might be unfriendly, but this Bean was even worse. I hadn't thought of Og all weekend. Now it all came back to me: the green skin, the repulsive grin, and the way he had leaped up and scared me. I had taken it from the frog, but I wasn't going to take it from this big bully.

This was the time to act!

I quickly opened the lock-that-doesn't-lock and took a deep breath before leaping onto Martin Bean's leg. "Stop being mean, Bean!" I yelled at the top of my voice. It may have sounded like squeaking to him, but I made my point.

"Eeek!" Marty shouted. "It's on me! A mouse!" He threw his hands up in the air and screamed as I ran in circles on his leg. "Help me, somebody! Help!"

The faces around me were a blur and I was getting dizzy. As Marty continued to scream, the other kids began to laugh, softly at first, then louder and louder.

"He's only a little hamster," I heard Garth say as he scooped me up in his hands. "He wouldn't hurt a flea."

I like being called a "he" a lot more than being called an "it."

"It tried to bite me!" Marty exclaimed. Everybody on the bus, including Beth and her first-grade friends, laughed.

"What is going on back there, Martin?" Miss Victoria called out as she slammed on the brakes.

"They—they threw a big rat on me!" He was almost in tears. "A giant rat!"

"I think you'd better come up and sit behind me," the bus driver said. "Now!" She had the girls in the seat behind her move as Marty shuffled to the front of the bus.

Garth put me back in my cage.

"Thanks, Humphrey," he whispered. "I don't know how you got out, but I'm sure glad you did."

"Always happy to help out a pal," I squeaked.

The rest of the ride was uneventful. When Miss Victoria stopped the bus in front of Longfellow School, she made an announcement. "This was the quietest ride we've ever had. From now on, Martin Bean, I'm assigning you the front seat. Permanently."

Marty didn't argue. He was in too much of a hurry to get off the bus. He could probably hear all the rest of the bus riders—including me—shouting, "Hooray!"

"No enemy can match a friend."

Jonathan Swift, Irish author

Rhyme Time

I felt pretty proud of myself after the bus ride. Once I was back in Room 26, I looked over at my pop-eyed neighbor.

"Morning, Og," I squeaked to him, hoping that after the long, lonely weekend he might be in a friendlier frame of mind. He responded to my greeting with dead silence and a grim grin. Or maybe he couldn't see me, because there was a huge piece of paper taped to the front of his glass box.

And something about that note must have been pretty funny, because all my classmates were laughing. Hard.

"All right, what's so funny?" asked Mrs. Brisbane.

"Og!" said Gail. She was giggling so hard I was afraid she'd get the hiccups again.

Mrs. Brisbane ripped the paper off the cage and read it. "Help! I'm a prince who's been turned into a frog. Kiss me quick!"

Somebody made loud smacking sounds, which made everyone laugh even louder. Mrs. Brisbane looked up from the paper. "I-Heard-That-Kirk. Are you volunteering to kiss Og?"

It was a pretty disgusting thought to me, but everyone else laughed.

"I think it has to be a girl," said Kirk.

Mrs. Brisbane folded up the paper. "Thank you for our joke of the day. You can Stop-Giggling-Gail. Now, let's all calm down and get to work. I'm anxious to hear the poems you've written, but let's get our spelling quiz out of the way first. Please take out a pencil and a piece of paper."

Whoops! I'd done a lot of thinking over the weekend. Something I hadn't thought about was our spelling quiz. Mrs. Brisbane and my classmates don't know that I usually slip into my sleeping house with my notebook and pencil and take the quizzes, too. I still hadn't gotten 100%, like Sayeh. I hoped I would someday.

This would not be the day.

I did all right with "practice," "jewel," and "pound." But "accommodate"? Did Mrs. Brisbane really think anyone except Sayeh would get that right? It looks like they threw in some extra letters left over from another word!

Next, it was time for the poems. "Kirk, you seem to want to be the center of attention this morning. You can go first."

Kirk jumped up and said, "I've got to write mine on the board."

Mrs. Brisbane told him to go ahead. When he was finished, he read it aloud.

"It's called 'Frog.' Here goes:

Funny
Ribbits
Oily
Green.
That's a frog.
Take away the funny ribbits
You've got Og!"

Mrs. Brisbane smiled and nodded her head. "Well done, Kirk. Very clever. What do you think, class?"

"Does that say 'oily'?" asked Repeat-It-Please-Richie. "Frogs aren't oily."

Kirk wrinkled his nose. "Well, he looks oily, even if he isn't. Besides, I need an O word to spell 'frog.' "

Mrs. Brisbane asked the class to help Kirk out with another O word. I decided to squeak up.

"Obnoxious! Offensive!" I yelled. I almost said "Unfriendly," but it doesn't begin with an O.

No one seemed to hear me. Sometimes I wish I had a big booming voice like A.J.'s.

" 'Honest'?" asked Seth, jumping up out of his seat.

"Sit-Still-Seth. That's a good guess, but 'honest' starts with a silent H." Mrs. Brisbane wrote the word on the board. Silent H—no fair! I'll have to watch out for that one.

"How about 'odd'?" suggested Art.

"What do you think, class? Do some people think frogs are odd?"

Some students nodded their heads. Nobody nodded harder than me.

"What do you think?" the teacher asked Kirk.

"Maybe 'oddball' fits him better," Kirk said, smiling. Everybody seemed to like the answer and I was not about to disagree.

I glanced over at Og to see what he thought. "Boing," he twanged. Everybody laughed, even Mrs. Brisbane.

"Oh, Og, you are so funny," she said.

Oddball, yes. Funny, no. In my humble opinion.

Heidi waved her hand in the air. "Og doesn't say 'Ribbit.' He goes 'Boing.' "

"R is for 'Boing'? Heidi, that makes 'Roing.' " Kirk looked very pleased with himself.

Heidi frowned. "That's not what I meant."

"That's enough on that one, Kirk. Why don't you work on it a little more?" said Mrs. Brisbane. She called for another volunteer. This time Heidi actually remembered to raise her hand. When the teacher called on her, she stood up and read her poem.

I met a little frog
And said, "How do you do?
My name is Hopper.
Is that your name, too?"
He croaked, "My name is Leaper.
That's what I do all day."

But when I tried to pick him up,
Leaper ran away.

"Nicely done, Heidi," said Mrs. Brisbane. "Good rhyming. It's a funny idea to use your own name. Anyone else?"

No hands were raised this time.

"How about you, Tabitha?" asked the teacher. "What did you write?"

Tabitha looked SCARED-SCARED-SCARED.

Mrs. Brisbane put on her friendliest smile. "Don't be afraid. We won't bite, will we, class?"

Most of the kids smiled and shook their heads. Kirk growled like a lion, just to be funny, but I couldn't tell if Tabitha noticed.

Slowly, she stood up and picked up her paper. In a soft voice, she read her poem like it was one sentence, really fast, like this:

"People-think-bears-are-mean-but-they've-never-seen-Smiley. He-doesn't-growl-or-make-you-sad-he-wouldn't-ever-be-bad-Smiley. I-don't-care-what-people-say-he-helps-me-get-through-the-day-Smiley."

Tabitha quickly sat down and stared at her table.

"Thank you, Tabitha. That's a lovely poem about a bear. And I liked the rhymes," said Mrs. Brisbane.

I saw Tabitha reach into her pocket and pat her stuffed bear.

I also saw Mandy look over at Heidi and roll her eyes. I could even read her lips as she mouthed the word "baby."

"Any volunteers?" asked the teacher. "Garth?"

Garth stood up to read his poem.

Roses are red,
Frogs are cool,
Now we've got one
Here at school.

He folded up his paper. "That's it."

Mrs. Brisbane reminded him that the poems were supposed to have six lines and Garth's poem had four.

Personally, I was in shock.

"Frogs are *cool*"? What kind of a poem is that? After *I* helped him and A.J. with Mean Bean, Garth wrote "*Frogs* are cool"?

We didn't have time for any more poems because the recess bell rang and my classmates raced to get their coats and gloves.

Tabitha took her time, waiting to see that no one was watching, and secretly stashed her bear in her pocket. Sayeh stayed behind, too, and approached her.

"I liked your poem. Is Smiley your bear's name?" she asked.

Tabitha nodded, but she didn't say anything. She didn't know how shy Sayeh was or how hard it was for her to come up and talk like that. But I knew.

"He's nice," said Sayeh. "Are you coming out to recess?"

Tabitha nodded again. Sayeh waited, but when

Tabitha didn't budge, she said, "See you outside," and hurried to the cloakroom with her head down, looking embarrassed.

I've got to admit, Speak-Up-Sayeh is a favorite friend of mine. To see Tabitha treat her that way made me MAD-MAD-MAD. She was about as friendly as a frog!

The new girl waited until everyone else had left the room before rising to get her coat.

Later, after the students left for the day, Miss Loomis came into Room 26, all bundled up in her coat, hat and gloves.

"Hi, Sue. I'm ready when you are," She walked over to Og's cage. "How's your star pupil doing?"

"Fine. He and Humphrey seem to get along all right. At least they don't disturb each other," said Mrs. Brisbane.

Don't disturb each other? I was pretty disturbed when Og leaped at me!

Mrs. Brisbane put on her coat. "Let's stop for coffee to warm us up on the way home."

"Sounds great," Miss Loomis answered. "I can't thank you enough for giving me a ride."

"What are friends for?" asked Mrs. Brisbane.

After they left, I felt as gloomy as the sky looked. Spinning my wheel warmed my fur up, but it didn't make me feel any warmer inside. What are friends for? For fun and talking and helping and sharing. Right?

"Hey, Og!" I called out, peering through the bars of

my cage at his glass house. "I hope you've been paying attention here in Room Twenty-six."

I waited a few seconds to allow him to answer, which he didn't, of course. "I hope you've seen what good friends the kids are. I mean, like Garth and A.J., the way they stick together. And Heidi and Gail, the way they like to giggle. Sayeh and Miranda are pals. Art and Richie, too. Wouldn't it be nice to have fun friends like them?"

I didn't actually expect an answer, of course, but this time I did get something: splashing. Splish-splash-splish. At least I knew Og was alive. Maybe he was even listening. I kept going. "Even if we can't actually talk to each other, we could—I don't know—have jumping contests." Suddenly, I had all kinds of ideas. "We could sing together. Or make funny faces at each other. Maybe you could teach me how to go 'Boing.' "

"Boing!"

I almost fainted. Was he answering me?

"Boing," I said, though I didn't sound much like a frog. "Boing to you, Og!"

"Boing-boing!" said Og.

"Yeah . . . boing!" I replied. My heart was thumping quite loudly. Were we actually having a conversation? "Uh . . . so what else is new?" I continued.

I waited, but there was no answer. "Og?" I called out. "Og, answer me!"

Silence. This was one frustrating frog. I tried again, but there were no more boings. Not even a splash. The room was silent as a tomb. That's about as quiet as it can get.

Somehow, it felt even worse to think that Og tried to talk to me and gave up. Still, Sayeh had learned a brand-new language when she came to this country. Maybe Og and I could learn to understand each other. I returned to my wheel and started spinning as fast as I could. I spun until it was almost dark.

At last, the door swung open and the lights came on.

"I have arrived!" Aldo announced, waving his broom. "No applause, please."

"HELLO-HELLO-HELLO!" I shouted. I was never so glad to see anybody in my life.

Aldo hurried toward my cage, rubbing his arms.

"Hey, it's cold in here. They turn the heat down at night to save money, but it's freezing outside. And it's almost freezing in here," said Aldo. He turned to Og's cage. "Hey, Og, how's the world treating you?"

When Og didn't answer him, Aldo turned back to me. "He's the strong, silent type, I guess. Say, Humph, old pal, I've been thinking. About that idea of getting a better job, you know? Maria thinks I should go back to school."

I tried to imagine Aldo sitting at a little table all day with Miranda, Richie and Seth. I didn't think his legs would fit.

"I could go to college during the day and still work here at night."

College! I hoped they had bigger chairs there.

Aldo pulled up a chair so we were practically whisker-to-whisker. "See, I went to college for a year. When my dad died, I quit because I needed to make money. I thought I'd go back, but I never did."

"It's never too late," I squeaked.

Aldo shook his head. "I'm not a kid anymore." He reached in his pocket. "Maria got me this application for City College, but I don't know."

City College! That's where Natalie the babysitter went! She said that's where people go to become doctors and lawyers and teachers. That's where people go to study things like psychology and get good jobs.

"GO-GO-GO!" I said, hopping up and down.

"Maria thinks I'm smart enough," said Aldo. "I just don't know if I can handle all that studying." He sighed and rose from his chair.

"Guess I'd better get this room cleaned or I won't have a job at all." Aldo tucked the application back in his pocket. "First, I'm going to go turn up the heat."

Good old Aldo. He was a thoughtful guy. And a smart guy, too. I hoped his wife could talk him into going back to school.

I wasn't sure I could do it all by myself. And I was pretty sure Og wouldn't be any help at all.

"One of the most beautiful qualities of true friendship is to understand and to be understood."

Seneca, Roman playwright

Crabby Abby

The next morning, Kirk hurried from the cloakroom and stuck a big piece of paper on my cage. It almost blocked my view of Og, which was not a bad thing.

Once the other students settled in their seats, they started giggling and pointing, led by Gail, of course. Mrs. Brisbane looked puzzled until she glanced over at my cage. The sign read, HELP! I'M BEING HELD PRISONER IN ROOM 26!

"And who is responsible for this, as if I didn't know?" she asked.

Kirk rose and took a bow as everyone applauded. I joined in, though I was the only one who knew I could never be a prisoner with my lock-that-doesn't-lock.

"Let's all sit down now," said Mrs. Brisbane. "And get back to poetry."

Somebody made a very, very rude noise and Mrs. Brisbane did not like that one little bit. "I-Heard-That-Kirk. And I don't ever want to hear it again."

During the rest of the week, we heard a lot more animal poems. Most of them were about frogs. One was about a dog (Miranda's). Sayeh wrote about a beautiful bird called a dove. ("Dove" rhymes with "love.")

Nobody wrote about hamsters.

Aldo didn't mention City College again. And Tabitha still didn't talk to anybody except Smiley.

I was looking forward to a change of scenery by the end of the week. A relaxing getaway to one of my classmates' cozy homes. One with plenty of heat and no frogs.

On Friday, Mrs. Brisbane said, "I can't remember. Who asked me about taking Humphrey home this weekend?" Miranda's hand shot up.

"Yes, Miranda. I got the note from your father. That will be fine."

I let out a little "Eek!" I don't think anyone heard me. Everyone knows that I have a special place in my hamster heart for Miranda. After all, her name is Golden and I am a Golden Hamster. We both have lovely golden hair.

But I have a terrible fear of her dog, Clem. I barely escaped a terrible fate the last time I went home with her, but could I do it again?

Then it hit me. "Wait a second! Did you say 'father'?" I squeaked. Because when I went home with Miranda before, there was only her mom. And the dog, of course. And Fanny the fish.

Mrs. Brisbane chuckled. "I guess Humphrey approves."

I puzzled over this all afternoon. Sure enough, at the end of the day, a tall man called Mr. Golden arrived to pick up his daughter. At least I wouldn't be riding the bus with Marty Bean—that was a break! Miranda, thoughtful as ever, threw a warm blanket over my cage. As they carried me out, Mrs. Brisbane picked up Og's cage.

"I thought you said Og stayed here on weekends," said Miranda.

Mrs. Brisbane chuckled. "It's a surprise for my husband. He always enjoys Humphrey, so I thought he'd get a kick out of having Og for the weekend."

I felt COLD-COLD-COLD and we were still inside! I thought the Brisbanes were my best friends of all. Were they ready to replace me with a frog?

Once we were in the car, I didn't have time to worry about the Brisbanes. I was too worried about facing Clem again. I could practically see his sloppy tongue and drippy nose and smell that bad breath waiting for me up in Miranda's apartment.

What a shock it was when the car pulled up in front of a house, not an apartment building. "Here we are, Humphrey," Miranda announced. "You've seen my mom's place, but this weekend we're staying at my dad's place."

A nice lady that Miranda called "Amy" met us at the door.

"Hi, honey," said Mr. Golden, kissing Amy on the cheek. "Meet Humphrey the hamster."

"Cute," Amy replied. "I think he should stay in the girls' room."

"What about the living room?" asked Miranda. "Or the dining room table?"

"I think he'd get in the way," Mr. Golden said. "Let's go to your room."

Miranda's room in the apartment had a bed, a desk, a fish tank and stars on the ceiling. Her room in this house had two beds, a dresser, a desk and no stars. Everything in this room was pink, from the walls to the bedspreads to the carpet on the floor. A girl about Miranda's age was sprawled across one bed, reading a magazine.

"What's THAT?" she asked in an unpleasant voice.

"Humphrey. He's our class hamster," Miranda explained.

"Well, he's not staying in my room," the girl stated firmly.

"It's Miranda's room, too, Abby," Amy said as she came in the door behind us. "Put Humphrey on the desk."

Miranda thoughtfully opened my cage to straighten out my ladder and my water bottle, which had slid around during the ride.

"Mom, I have to do homework on that desk," said Abby, sitting up.

Huh? Amy was Abby's mom and she was married to Miranda's dad? Things were quite confusing.

"Okay, we'll put his cage on the floor," said Amy.

I heard a baby crying in another room. "I've got to see what Ben wants," she said. Mr. Golden followed her and Abby got up to close the door.

"He stays on your side of the room," Abby told Miranda. "And don't forget, no crossing the line."

Abby took her foot and dragged it in a straight line across the middle of the pink carpet. "No crossing the line. Ever."

Miranda sighed. "I know. You tell me every time I'm here."

"Sometimes you forget. And don't touch anything of mine."

"I never do," Miranda countered.

"You used my barrette last time," said Abby.

"It was a mistake! It looks exactly like mine!" Good for Miranda for standing up for herself! "I didn't complain when you borrowed my book without asking."

Abby plopped back on the bed again and thumbed through her magazine. "Just don't cross the line," she muttered.

I hopped on my wheel for a spin. Sometimes it cheers people up to watch me spinning. Abby was not one of those people. She glared at me. "Don't tell me it makes noise," she said nastily. "Can't you stop it?"

"Humphrey is not an 'it.' He's a 'he.'" said Miranda. I love that girl! "You could read in the living room," she suggested.

"I was here first." Abby suddenly slammed down her magazine and stood up. "Okay, anything to get away from you."

After she left, Miranda leaned down close to my cage. "I was hoping she'd like you, Humphrey. She sure doesn't like me. It's not my fault my dad married her mom. It's not my fault she has to share her room with me every other weekend." She sighed. "I've tried to be friends with her, but it's no use. She's a wicked stepsister, like in *Cinderella*."

Miranda looked SAD-SAD-SAD, so I leaped up on my ladder and hung from it by one paw to cheer her up.

She smiled, so I leaped onto my tree and began swinging from branch to branch, like that Tarzan guy I saw on TV. That made Miranda laugh.

Abby returned with a sour expression on her face. I must have looked that way the day somebody in Room 26 (I'm still trying to figure out who) slipped me a slice of lemon.

"Mom wants us to help fix dinner. She's got to feed the baby."

She disappeared as quickly as she had appeared.

"See you, Humphrey," Miranda whispered. "And remember, don't cross the line!"

After she left, I squinted my eyes, but I couldn't see a line anywhere. All I could see was a sea of pink. So much pink, I felt a little ill.

Later that night, while Miranda took her bath, I was alone with Abby. I decided to try and be friendly.

"Nice room you've got," I squeaked politely.

Abby turned toward me and frowned. "Were you squeaking at me?" She shook her head. "This is the last straw. First, I have a room all to myself. Then Mom marries *him* and pretty soon I have a stepsister taking half my room and a new baby brother crying all the time and nobody knows I exist! I'm supposed to be happy about the whole thing when it wasn't *my* idea. And now they've moved in a guinea pig!"

That wasn't a huge insult, because guinea pigs are cute and furry like me, only not quite *as* cute. Anyway, I could see Abby's point. I wasn't happy about Og moving into Room 26 and it sure wasn't my idea! The difference was, Miranda is actually nice. And Og is, well, Og.

Miranda returned and the two girls settled into their respective beds.

"Night, Humphrey," Miranda said to me.

Neither girl said a word to the other.

I had a long night ahead of me, and since I'm nocturnal and do most of my sleeping during the day, I had a lot of time to think.

What Abby had told me helped me understand why she was so crabby with Miranda. If only I'd studied psychology like Natalie, maybe I could get inside her head and figure out how to make her like Miranda as much as I did.

The next morning, Miranda cleaned my cage while Abby lounged on the bed, writing in her diary.

"What are you doing, anyway?" she asked Miranda.

"Taking out the old bedding, putting in new. Changing the water, stuff like that."

Abby slammed her diary shut. "It doesn't—you know—go to the *bathroom* in there, does it?"

"Well, sure."

Abby leaped off her bed and pointed to the door. "That's the most disgusting thing I've ever heard. Get it out of my room right now!"

(I've figured out a lot about humans, but I still don't know why my little potty corner is always such a big deal to them. I'm really quite tidy.)

Miranda didn't budge. "He's on my side of the room."

I was all for Miranda. On the other paw, I could see that Abby had been through a lot of changes in a short time. It's not easy getting a new roommate. I learned that the hard way! I also knew what a good friend Miranda can be. Friends help friends, so I figured it was time I did something about it.

I had a Plan. A Plan using reverse psychology. Since Miranda had no luck getting Abby to like her, my Plan would make them *not* like each other even more. (If that was possible.)

Okay, it didn't make a lot of sense, but when Natalie used reverse psychology, it worked REALLY-REALLY-REALLY well.

I had the chance to set my Plan in motion a short time later when Mr. Golden announced that the whole family was going to a museum.

"Do we *all* have to go?" asked Abby.

"Yes, all of us. We're a family, you know," said her mom.

Abby wrinkled her nose. "Even the baby?"

"We'll bring the stroller," said Miranda's dad. "He'll like it."

Despite her grumbling, Abby joined the rest of the family and I soon had the whole house to myself. My Plan would take speed, strength, courage and lots of time. It would be well worth it . . . IF it worked.

Once I was sure they were gone, I opened the lock-that-doesn't-lock and hurried over to Abby's bed. I had been studying it all morning and thought that if I grabbed on, I could climb the bedspread, paw over paw, like a rope. I was huffing and puffing by the time I reached the top, but I made it! Sitting on top of the bedspread was the purple-and-pink striped pen Abby used to write in her diary. I gave it a big push and it rolled off the bed and onto the floor.

After that, I scrambled over to Abby's night table. There, I found her pink bracelet with ABBY spelled out in purple and white beads. I pushed that onto the floor, too.

The next part of my mission was fun. I grabbed the edge of the bedspread and slid DOWN-DOWN-DOWN really fast!

I was far from finished. Next I climbed all the way up Miranda's bedspread to get to her gold ring with the pink stone, which I pushed onto the floor, along with a red loopy thing she sometimes used to pull back her hair. (You don't expect a guy hamster to know what it's called!)

I was halfway to my goal, and the hardest part of my Plan was yet to come.

All morning, I'd had my eye on a big ball of string on

the desk. A long piece of the string hung down almost to the floor. I grabbed it and pulled as hard as I could. More and more string unrolled and fell to the floor. I chewed it off and set to work.

Looping the string around the pen and the bracelet, then holding the string in my teeth, I climbed up Miranda's bedspread again. Whew! Mrs. Brisbane says exercise is good for you, but that was work! Once I was on the bed, I tugged on the string, pulling up the pen and the bracelet. (Believe me, for a small hamster, those two items are very heavy!) I carefully laid them both on Miranda's pillow where she couldn't miss them.

As tired as I was, there was no time to rest. I slid down to the floor, looped the string around Miranda's ring and the hair holder and pulled them up onto Abby's bed, laying them on her pillow.

(I'm happy to say those two items were not as heavy as the others.)

When the girls came back, Miranda would find Abby's belongings on her own pillow. Abby would find Miranda's things on her own pillow.

I scurried back to my cozy cage and closed the door behind me. I wanted to be safe when the fireworks began!

"Little friends may prove to be great friends."

Aesop, writer of fables

Fright Night

Abby entered first, plopped down on her bed as usual, and sighed a big sigh.

"THAT was fun," she said. "Especially when the baby spit up in the restaurant." I don't think she was actually talking to me, but I listened anyway.

A second later, Miranda came in. "Hi, Humphrey. Did you miss me?" she asked, bending down close to my cage.

"Of course!" I squeaked.

"I suppose you understand what it's saying," Abby said sourly.

"Sort of," said Miranda. "I think he's trying to tell me he missed me."

Bingo!

I watched Abby closely as she reached for her diary and pen. "Where's my pen?" she asked. She looked at her pillow. "What's this stuff doing here?"

Miranda pointed at Abby's bed. "Hey, that's my hair scrunchie!"

So that's what the hair thing is called!

"And my ring!" Miranda jumped up, crossed over the imaginary line and grabbed her things. "You took them!"

Abby spotted something on Miranda's pillow. "There's my pen! You took it! And my name bracelet!" She snatched her items and glared at Miranda. "You're always taking my things."

"You took *my* things! I never touched yours," Miranda insisted. I never heard her sound that angry before.

Abby's face turned red. "Why would I take your dinky ring and your stupid scrunchie? I have my own ring and my own scrunchie!"

"Why would I take your dumb pen and a bracelet with *your* name on it? And why would I put them on my pillow where you can see them?" asked Miranda.

"Just to be mean?"

"I'm not mean!" said Miranda. "Anyway, isn't it weird that my things were on your pillow and your things were on my pillow?"

Abby thought for a moment. "Like somebody planned it."

"Like somebody wanted us to notice," agreed Miranda.

Suddenly, they were actually talking instead of arguing. I crossed my paws. This had to work!

Abby sat back down on her bed. "Who would do that? My mom wouldn't. Or your dad."

Miranda collapsed onto her bed. "Well, the baby didn't do it." She started to giggle.

"Maybe Humphrey did it," said Abby, and she started to giggle.

I chuckled, too.

"Those things didn't fly from bed to bed," said Miranda. "Somebody put them there on purpose."

"Or some*thing*," said Abby. "Like a . . . a ghost!"

Miranda turned pale. "You don't have ghosts here, do you?"

"No," said Abby, shaking her head. "At least I don't think we do."

"There are no such things as ghosts," insisted sensible Miranda. She sounded like she was trying to convince herself.

"NO-NO-NO, there aren't any ghosts, except in stories," I squeaked. I *know* I was trying to convince myself.

"I know," said Abby. She opened her diary and tore out a page. "I'll write down every possibility of who could have done this. Number one: Miranda."

"I didn't!" Miranda protested.

"I'm just writing down all the possibilities. Miranda, me, my mom, your dad, Ben, Humphrey. They're the only ones in the house—right? Unless there was a burglar."

The fur on my back stood straight up. Burglars are scary things!

"Burglars break windows and steal things," Miranda pointed out. "The doors were locked, the windows were locked and nothing was stolen."

"I'm writing all this down. Burglar. Ghost." Abby quietly stared at the paper for a moment. "Would you swear you didn't do it?"

"Of course," said Miranda.

"And I'd swear I didn't do it. Hey, wait a second! Maybe it *was* Humphrey!" Abby jumped up and walked over to my cage. She bent down and checked the door. "Nope. It couldn't be him because his door is locked."

Thank goodness that old lock-that-doesn't-lock fools them every time!

"The only thing on the list that makes sense is a ghost," she announced.

"But it doesn't make sense," said Miranda.

"I know," Abby agreed.

The girls actually agreed on something. This was progress! They'd gone from not liking each other to being REALLY-REALLY-REALLY mad, to talking things over.

After a while, the girls left the room to have dinner. This time, they left together. When they came back much later, they were still together.

"Dad said it didn't make sense," Miranda was saying.

"And Mom agreed," Abby replied. "What now?"

The girls flopped down on their respective beds. "I know," said Abby. "Let's stay up all night."

"Why?"

"To see if any ghosts show up."

I felt a chill creep down my spine. I knew I was the one who moved their things around. And I knew I wasn't a ghost. But I still got a shiver thinking something SCARY-SCARY-SCARY just might show up.

"Lights out, ladies." Mr. Golden stood at the door later that night, smiling. "Hope you have sweet dreams. You, too, Humphrey."

"Thanks!" I squeaked back.

"Everybody all tucked in?" Amy appeared at the door, holding baby Ben.

"Yes, Mom." Abby snuggled down in her bed and pulled up the covers.

"Good night," said Miranda, pulling up her blanket as well.

The lights went out and it was DARK-DARK-DARK in the room, except for the night-light in the wall, which gave off a pink glow.

The girls were quiet for a few minutes. Then Abby whispered, "Are you awake?"

"Yes," Miranda whispered back.

"Know any scary stories?" asked Abby.

I certainly knew a few. Like about the time Clem, the dog, almost ate me. Or the time Aldo first came in the room at night and I thought *he* was a ghost.

Miranda thought for a minute and said, "I remember one from camp."

"Tell it," said Abby. "But not too loud."

Miranda—sweet Golden-Miranda—told a fur-raising tale about a hitchhiker who turned out to be a ghost. The way she told it was scarier than facing Clem!

"That was a good one," said Abby. "I know one, too."

Her story was even worse. It was about a group of kids who dared each other to go into a graveyard at night. One girl went in, saw a horrible face and died of fright. Recalling Og's gruesome grin, I felt faint after that story!

"Abby?" Miranda whispered. "Maybe we shouldn't tell any more scary stories. I'm feeling kind of weird."

"Me, too," said Abby. "Let's be quiet."

It was quiet all right. Maybe a little too quiet for a nocturnal fellow like me. Without thinking, I hopped on my wheel for some exercise. I guess that wheel needs oil, because it went *SCREEEECH!*

When the wheel screeched, both girls screamed, "EEEEEE!" By the little pink light, I could see them leap from their beds and wrap their arms around each other.

The door abruptly swung open and the big light came on.

"EEEEEE!" the girls screamed again.

"It's just me," said Mr. Golden, rushing in. "What's going on?"

He must have been as surprised as I was to see Miranda and Abby hugging one another for dear life.

"There was this terrible noise!" said Abby.

"Horrible," said Miranda.

That was my cue to hop back on the wheel. *SCREEEECH!*

All eyes were on me.

"You mean that noise?" said Miranda's dad, pointing at my cage.

"That's the one," I squeaked.

Both girls started giggling.

"It was Humphrey," said Miranda.

"I thought it was a ghost," said Abby.

Mr. Golden laughed, too. "I think that ghost is pretty harmless," he said. "Now, do you think you two—or you three—can get some sleep?"

They agreed and he tucked the girls into their beds.

"It's good to hear you two laughing, but no more screaming, okay?" he said as he turned out the light.

The girls were quiet for a while longer and I stayed away from the wheel. I heard Abby whisper, "Miranda, could you sleep over here with me, just for tonight?"

"I was going to ask you the same thing," said Miranda.

Miranda crawled into bed with Abby.

"Did you ever hear the story about the ghost in the attic?" Abby whispered.

"Tell it," said Miranda.

And she did. I couldn't have slept that night, even if I wasn't nocturnal.

On Sunday morning, neither girl mentioned how the ring and the bracelet, the pen and the hair scrunchie all got moved. Neither girl mentioned an imaginary line, either. They did their homework at the desk, braided each other's hair and made a maze for me to run.

And when they said good-bye on Monday morning, Miranda said, "See you in two weeks."

Abby said, "Great!"

"All things are in common among friends."

Diogenes, Greek philosopher

Ill Will

I returned to school with a great sense of accomplishment.

But once I remembered where Og had spent the last two days, it was hard to concentrate on geography or math. I couldn't help imagining all the fun Og must have had with the Brisbanes. I glanced over at my neighbor in his glass tank. With that horrible grin on his face, he looked like a jack-o-lantern. (Scary.)

It was VERY-VERY-VERY cold outside, which meant that the heat inside was turned way, way up. Whew! That must be fine for a cold-blooded amphibian, but I was wishing I could take off my fur coat. Then the warm air woke up the crickets, who started singing. And there was a SQUEAK-SQUEAK-SQUEAK that was not coming from me, but from Seth as he wiggled in his chair. It sounded like "Jingle Bells": Squeak-squeak-squeak . . . squeak-squeak-squeak . . . squeak-SQUEAK-squeak-squeak-squeak! The squeaking made Gail giggle noisily, which made Mrs. Brisbane loudly shush her. I was looking forward to some peace and quiet during recess (knowing Og wouldn't want to chat). But when the time came, Mrs. Brisbane announced that the class would stay inside. She brought out all kinds of interesting things to play with. I must admit, I wished I could get out of my cage and play along with the rest of the class.

Art and Richie built a tall tower out of tiny bricks while Kirk and Seth worked on a jigsaw puzzle. A.J. and Garth played a game where you slapped down cards. Heidi and Gail played another kind of game, moving little plastic men around a board. Mandy, Sayeh and Miranda came over to ask Tabitha to play with them. She didn't even look up. She just shook her head.

"I don't know why we even try to be friends with her," Mandy whispered to the other girls.

Sayeh just sighed sadly. I knew how she felt.

"Og, can you hear me?" I squeaked. "I have something to ask you." I figured even though I couldn't understand him, maybe he could understand me.

"See how much fun it is to play with your friends?" I asked. It probably sounded like "Squeak-squeak-squeak," but he could have at least responded with a "Boing!"

I decided to squeak up louder this time. I couldn't even hear myself because of all the yelling.

Yelling?

I looked around to see who was making all that noise. It wasn't Lower-Your-Voice-A.J. or Repeat-It-Please-Richie. It was Gail. She had stopped giggling and started shouting. The person she was shouting at was her best friend, Heidi.

"You cheated! I saw you!" she yelled.

"I didn't," Heidi said. "I wouldn't cheat."

"You must have. You always win. I'm never playing with you again, cheater," Gail shouted.

Mrs. Brisbane quickly moved toward them. "Girls, please!"

"I didn't cheat," insisted Heidi. "I'm not a cheater."

Gail put her fingers in her ears. "Did too, cheater, cheater, cheater!"

Everyone else in the class stopped playing and stared at the two girls. Mrs. Brisbane was right between them now. "Girls, please calm down and be quiet."

Heidi and Gail were quiet, but they glared at each other angrily.

"Tell me what happened, Gail. Calmly."

Gail wiped away some tears. "She was supposed to move her man five spaces and she moved it six spaces. That gave her a bonus jump and she won. She cheated!"

"Did not!" Heidi shouted. "I only went five!"

The teacher held up both hands. "Stop. I want you two to cool off before we talk about it. You're such good friends, let's work this out."

"She's not my friend anymore!" said Gail. She was crying harder.

"Thank goodness!" Heidi shot back. "Because I can't stand you! Crybaby!"

"Cheater!"

Mrs. Brisbane shook her head. "Heidi, you go over there by Humphrey and Og," she said firmly. "Gail, you go sit at my desk. Try and settle down."

The girls did as they were told. I think they were glad to get away from each other. Soon, Heidi was leaning up against the table where Og and I have our homes.

"Crybaby," she whispered so softly, only we could hear her.

It was hard for me to believe that Heidi would cheat her best friend. It was hard for me to believe that Gail would lie about Heidi. I thought friends always got along, no matter what.

"First, all she does is giggle. Now all she does is cry," Heidi muttered.

At Mrs. Brisbane's desk, Gail glared over at Heidi and wiped away a few more tears.

When recess was almost over, Mrs. Brisbane took the two girls out into the hall to discuss the argument. They came back in and quietly returned to their seats. But as soon as Mrs. Brisbane turned her back, I saw them stick their tongues out at each other. Maybe friendship wasn't all it was cracked up to be.

It was snowing by afternoon recess, so Mrs. Brisbane divided the class into four teams. Each team had questions to answer. They had to decide as a group what the answer should be. Mrs. Brisbane kept score.

She wisely put Heidi and Gail on different teams so they wouldn't argue or make faces. Both their teams lost.

The winning team had Miranda, Kirk, Seth and

Tabitha on it. And, to my surprise, the reason they won was Tabitha!

Mrs. Brisbane asked each team questions about all kinds of things: flowers, books, poetry, sports, animals (but not hamsters, I'm sorry to say) and countries. Nobody knew much about flowers. Everybody knew a lot about animals. Sayeh was the best at answering questions about countries. (Would you believe there's a country with a capital called Tegucigalpa? I had to write that one down.)

But Tabitha was the best at answering questions about sports. She knew soccer teams, volleyball rules and golf champions. The boys all seemed amazed. As the quiz went on, there seemed to be more and more questions about sports. Maybe that was an accident, but when Mrs. Brisbane is involved, things don't usually happen by chance.

By the end of the recess period, Tabitha's team had scored forty points. They would have scored even higher if Kirk hadn't said that the Gettysburg Address was the number on the Gettysburg family home. (Even I know it was a speech written by a very famous president.) He got a laugh and lost two points, but it didn't matter. The next closest team only had twenty-eight points.

"We won!" yelled Seth, the team captain. "Way to go!" He high-fived Tabitha, Miranda and Kirk.

"Three cheers for Tabitha!" said Miranda.

"Hip-hip-hooray! Hip-hip-hooray! Hip-hip-hooray!" I squeaked, jumping up and down for joy.

Nobody called her a baby. Even Tabitha looked happy.

Unfortunately, Heidi and Gail didn't seem cheered up at all. In fact, while all the attention was focused on Tabitha, I saw Gail mouth "cheater" to Heidi.

Heidi stuck her tongue out at Gail.

It was enough to make a grown hamster cry. A less sensible hamster than me, of course.

"Og, you may not understand me, but if you could, you'd want Heidi and Gail to be friends again. Right?" I asked my neighbor once everyone had gone home for the day. I didn't expect him to understand me. I was just thinking out loud.

I was amazed to get an answer: "BOING!"

Og jumped straight up and down, up and down, over and over again. I didn't know if he had sat on a tack or eaten something that didn't agree with him.

"Og! Are you all right?"

"BOING-BOING!" he said. "BOING!"

I jumped up and looked over at him. I was pretty sure he was agreeing with me!

"So what are we going to do?" I asked him. "How can we help them?"

As abruptly as he began, Og stopped bouncing and boinging and sat as still as a rock, as usual. I was discouraged and puzzled, too. Either he didn't have any ideas or he'd given up on trying to get me to understand him. I felt we both had failed.

Finally, I spoke again. "They sure were good friends."

Og stayed silent the rest of the night.

Hours later, when Aldo arrived, I was still trying to figure out what google-eyes had been trying to tell me. This was a most peculiar frog.

"Good evening, gentlemen. Mind if I join the party?" said Aldo as he flicked on the lights and rolled his cleaning cart into Room 26.

"Without you, there is no party," I told him.

"Speaking of parties, Richie is having a big party for his birthday soon." Repeat-It-Please-Richie Rinaldi happened to be Aldo's nephew. "It's going to be a very big deal."

Since I had never been to one, any birthday party sounded special to me.

"They're having entertainment, like a show or something. Hey, you guys want to see my latest trick?" asked Aldo, grabbing his broom.

The custodian had already proved his talents to me by balancing his broom on the tip of one finger for a LONG-LONG-LONG time. Once, he balanced it on top of his head.

This time, he threw his head back and balanced the tip end of the broom on his chin for an equally long period of time. When the broom finally wobbled too far, Aldo caught it and took a deep bow.

"Bravo, Aldo!" I squeaked as loudly as I could.

"Thank you, Humph." He glanced at Og. "What's the matter, Froggy? You don't like tricks?"

"It's not you," I said softly. "It's him."

Aldo grabbed his lunch and pulled a chair close to my cage. "Aw, it's just a silly trick. I'm not good at anything useful."

"Not true!" I argued.

Aldo took a sandwich out of his bag and began chewing on it.

"No, Humph, I've been thinking about it a lot. Because of this." He pulled a piece of paper out of his pocket.

"This is the application for City College. If I want to go there, I have to fill it out. So I wrote my name, address, all that. When I got to the part that asked what I want to study, I got stuck," he explained. "I'm practically middle-aged and I still don't know what I want to be when I grow up." Aldo put down his sandwich and stared at the application.

"I'm not sure what I'm good at. I thought of being a teacher, but I don't know. Would the kids like me? Am I smart enough to be a really good teacher?"

"Yes! Be a teacher! Please!" I insisted. For once, Aldo didn't seem to hear me.

"Besides, they want a letter of recommendation from somebody important. Somebody who believes I can succeed," said Aldo.

"I'll do it!" I assured him, but he wasn't paying attention.

"I'm just not sure." He tossed his lunch bag back onto the cart. "Don't think I forgot you, pal," he told me as he dropped a small piece of carrot in my cage.

"Thanks a heap!" I squeaked.

"You're welcome," Aldo replied.

At least *he* understood most of what I said. One thing I understood: It was time for me to take action!

"Never injure a friend, even in jest."

Cicero, Roman writer and orator

9

Mrs. Brisbane Explains

After the custodian left, I noticed something odd beside my cage. Aldo was usually good at picking up things that didn't belong in the classroom. However, this night, he had left something behind: his City College application. I opened the good old lock-that-doesn't-lock and slipped out of my cage.

"Don't worry, Oggy old boy. I won't bother you if you won't bother me," I assured him. Maybe I was reassuring myself he wouldn't leap at me again.

The application was a big piece of paper that folded up. Half of it was stuck under my cage, and it was hard to read what Aldo had written. If you're a small hamster, human handwriting looks HUGE-HUGE-HUGE. The only light I had to read by was from the streetlamp outside the window. I squinted my eyes and I could read: AREA OF STUDY. On the line next to it, Aldo had written "Teaching" and scratched it out.

On the line marked RECOMMENDATION, he hadn't written anything.

I was tempted to get out my little pencil and write a nice recommendation myself. But a big college probably wouldn't care about the opinion of a small hamster, even a classroom hamster who could read and write. No, Aldo needed help from someone a lot bigger and more important than me.

I knew who that person was. I just hoped she would help.

I pulled the application out farther and neatly left it right between my cage and Og's.

"No splashing over here, Og," I warned my neighbor. "We want to keep this application in good shape."

He didn't splash all night long. Who knows—maybe Og understood me after all, even without ears.

I could hardly wait for Mrs. Brisbane to arrive the following morning. When she finally showed up, it took her a long time to take off her coat and gloves and arrange her desk. At last, she strolled—slowly—over to my cage.

"Morning, Humphrey," she said with a smile. "You're lucky you don't have to go out in this freezing-cold weather. You can stay right here in your cozy cage."

Stay in my cage? If she only knew!

She turned to Og. "Morning, Og. As you've heard in class, amphibians are cold-blooded, which means we've got to keep you warm."

She smiled at Og and turned away.

"Wait! Stop!" I shouted, jumping up and down. "Look at the paper!"

She turned back and laughed. "What's the matter, Humphrey? Are you jealous of Og?" She leaned closer. "You know you're my favorite hamster. And you mustn't let jealousy, that old green-eyed monster, get the best of you."

Eeek—a monster? I was about to dive into my sleeping house for protection, but then I remembered that jealousy is when you envy somebody else. Jealousy wasn't a real monster, just a giant bad feeling. Was that why I felt bad when everybody else paid attention to Og? I wasn't sure. After all, my eyes are brown, not green. I was trying to sort it all out when Mrs. Brisbane turned to walk away.

I'd forgotten something REALLY-REALLY-REALLY important!

"The application!" I shouted. I knew all she'd hear was squeaking, but I had to try.

Mrs. Brisbane came back to the cage. "For goodness' sake, calm down, Humphrey."

I didn't calm down. I started squeaking and jumping, jumping and squeaking, because I couldn't think of anything else to do . . . except open the cage door and hand her the application.

I couldn't do that because she'd find out about the lock-that-doesn't-lock.

"What's this?" Mrs. Brisbane picked up the application—whew!—and started to read! "Aldo must have left this here by mistake. I'll put it in his mailbox."

She folded it up without finishing it.

"Tell her, Og! Help me . . . help Aldo!" I was shrieking more than squeaking now, and to my amazement, Og let out a rather large "BOING!" which I really appreciated.

"What's the matter with you two? It's an application. It's private."

"BOING! BOING!"

"SQUEAK-SQUEAK-SQUEAK!"

Working together, we kept up the noisemaking and Mrs. Brisbane looked confused. She opened the application and started reading, thank goodness, because I was getting quite hoarse.

"Well, well. Aldo is applying to go back to college. That's a good idea. And he wants to study . . ." She stopped and stared a bit longer. "He wrote in 'Teaching,' but he crossed it out again. I wonder why?"

"Ask him!" I shouted with the last bit of my voice.

"I'd better give Aldo a call," said Mrs. Brisbane.

"Hi, Mrs. Brisbane!" a loud voice yelled. It was Lower-Your-Voice-A.J.

Mrs. Brisbane greeted him and folded up the application. She took it to her desk and didn't look at it again all day.

There was nothing to do now but keep my paws firmly crossed, which I did.

Sometime in the afternoon, I must have dozed off, but I was awakened by a now-familiar noise. "Chirrup!" That was the sound of a cricket. This time, it was coming from the middle of the room.

"Mrs. Brisbane?" a voice called out.

"Chirrup!"

Our teacher turned away from the board, where she was writing out a math problem. "Yes, Kirk?"

"I think a cricket got loose." Kirk pointed to the floor near his table.

"Well, pick it up, please," Mrs. Brisbane said.

"Chirrup! Chirrup!"

Kirk bent down and cupped his hands, touching the floor. "I've got it!"

"Good. Now please put it back where it belongs."

Kirk lifted his hands and sat upright in his chair. "I don't know, Mrs. Brisbane. I think it might get away."

Everyone was watching as Kirk stood up and started walking toward the cabinet where the crickets were kept. As he passed by Heidi, he suddenly opened his hands up right over her head. "Oops! Dropped it. Sorry, Heidi."

Heidi leaped up and started jumping around the room, shaking her head and running her hands through her hair. "Help! Get it off me. Get it off!" she screamed.

Everyone was laughing. Everyone except Mrs. Brisbane.

"Kirk Chen, you find that cricket," she said in a very stern tone of voice. "Now!"

Kirk grinned. "Aw, there was no cricket. I was making that noise."

Heidi stopped jumping around and glared at him.

"Hear it? Chirrup. Chirrup." Kirk really sounded like

a cricket. "Boy, that Heidi Hopper sure can hop!" he added.

Gail giggled until Heidi shot her a very angry look, then quickly covered her mouth to stop herself.

Mrs. Brisbane slowly walked toward Kirk. "You, my friend, are in trouble. Big trouble," she said. "You will stay in during recess and we'll have a little talk."

As Kirk returned to his seat, the room was very quiet. Except for a loud "Chirrup!"

Without even turning to look at him, Mrs. Brisbane said, "I-Heard-That-Kirk Chen."

I wouldn't have wanted to be Kirk when it was time for recess. Once the other students had cleared out, Mrs. Brisbane marched over to him. Boy, was he in trouble! So I was surprised at the first thing she said.

"I have a confession to make. I think you're a funny guy, Kirk. You make me laugh a lot. Someday, you might star in a funny movie, and I promise you, I'll be the first one in line to buy a ticket."

Kirk looked as confused as I felt.

"But . . ." Uh-oh, here came the clincher. "There's a time to be funny and a way to be funny that's appropriate. And there's a time to be funny and a way to be funny that is not. It's time for you to learn the difference."

I waited for a "Chirrup," or at least an argument, but Kirk remained silent.

"Why did you pretend to drop a cricket on Heidi's head?" Mrs. Brisbane asked.

Kirk shrugged his shoulders. "Because it was funny?"

"Do you think Heidi thought it was funny?"

Kirk shook his head.

"I think you did it to get attention. And if that's the case, it worked." I'm not sure, but I think Mrs. Brisbane smiled. "Now, why do you like to get attention?"

Kirk shrugged again.

"So people will like you?" the teacher asked.

"Maybe."

"Then I have good news for you. You don't have to play pranks anymore. People already like you. You're one of the most popular students I have."

I'm not sure, but I think Kirk smiled a little, too.

"So the next time you think of doing something funny, I want you to think about two things. First: Is it really funny? Or is it hurtful to someone? Second: Are you just doing it to get attention? Can you work on that?"

"Yes, ma'am," said Kirk.

"Because if you continue to act like you acted today, I'm afraid you're going to be doing a solo comedy act in Principal Morales' office. And he may not think you're funny at all."

I think Mr. Morales has a good sense of humor. But I also think that Mrs. Brisbane is good at figuring out what's going in people's heads. I bet she studied psychology in college.

Kirk was quiet for the rest of the day. So were Og and the crickets.

After my classmates went home, Mrs. Brisbane hung around longer than usual. I soon learned why. Aldo came to Room 26 to see her.

"Mrs. Brisbane, thanks for your call," he said.

"And I thank you for coming in early to talk," she said.

They looked funny sitting in those little student chairs.

"I hope you'll forgive me for reading this application you left behind. It was none of my business," she explained.

Maybe not, but I'd made sure it *was* her business, with a little help from Og.

"When I saw that you had written in 'Teaching' and then crossed it out, I thought perhaps you'd like to talk."

"Yes, I would," said Aldo. He was strangely quiet, and I guess he was nervous, because he kept tugging at his collar. "I was thinking I'd like to be a teacher, but I'm kind of . . . afraid."

Mrs. Brisbane listened while Aldo explained his fears about not being smart enough or interesting enough to be a good teacher.

"Everybody feels that way," she said with a warm smile. "What makes you think you would like to teach?"

Was I surprised to hear Aldo talk about how much he liked books, science, history, math, learning . . . how much he liked children! (He didn't mention hamsters, but I knew how he felt about me.)

When he was finished, Mrs. Brisbane laughed out

loud. "You'd better become a teacher or I'll be angry with you. You sound like a born teacher!"

"How can I know for sure?" Aldo asked.

"Would you like to try it out?" Mrs. Brisbane asked.

"Try out . . . teaching?"

"Yes. We'll pick a day for you to come in and teach a subject to the class. You can pick any subject. See how it feels to be in front of a classroom. See how the students react to you."

Aldo rose and began to pace. "That's a wonderful offer. I don't know. Sounds good. Maybe."

"Please think about it, talk it over with your wife, and let me know," Mrs. Brisbane suggested. "But you'll have to do it soon. This application is due in a week."

"I will, I will," said Aldo. "If I could be half the teacher you are, I'd be happy."

Mrs. Brisbane laughed. "Thank you, Aldo. But even after all these years, I still have my bad days."

Aldo shook her hand about ten times before leaving.

Mrs. Brisbane gathered together her things, and when she was ready to leave for the day, she turned to Og and me. "Hope you're satisfied, guys," she said.

I don't know about Og, but believe me, I was HAPPY-HAPPY-HAPPY.

I wasn't surprised that Mrs. Brisbane helped Aldo. It happened just the way I planned it. But the next day, I had a big surprise I never could have planned.

My classmates were all hurrying out of Room 26,

heading for the lunchroom. Usually, Sit-Still-Seth would have raced out of the room. But on this day, he hung behind the others.

"Coming?" Kirk asked impatiently.

"Meet you there," said Seth.

Seth was the only student left in the room except for Tabitha, who was trying to stuff Smiley into her pocket as Seth approached.

I couldn't imagine what he was doing. Tabitha had given the girls the cold shoulder when they tried to be friends. And Seth is a boy. Everybody knows boys and girls can't be friends. At least, that's what I heard Art and Richie say.

"How'd you know all that sports stuff the other day?" he asked her.

Tabitha shrugged her shoulders. "I don't know. I just like sports. And I remember things I hear about sports."

"Me, too," answered Seth. "What sports do you like best?"

Tabitha thought about it. "Basketball and baseball. Football. Tennis."

"Me, too," Seth agreed.

Mrs. Brisbane was in the doorway. "Are you two coming?"

"Right away," said Seth. But he turned back to Tabitha. "Listen, I've got to ask. Why do you keep that dumb bear with you? Aren't you too old for that?" he asked.

Tabitha shrugged again.

"When I was little, back in first grade, I had a truck I used to bring to school with me. I couldn't stand to be without it," Seth told her.

"Do you still have it?" asked Tabitha.

"It's in my closet. Sometimes I take it out, but I don't bring it to school anymore."

Mrs. Brisbane waited at the door. Now she didn't seem to be in such a hurry to get to lunch.

"My mom gave me Smiley," Tabitha explained. "My real mom. I haven't seen her for four years."

"Oh," said Seth. "I get it."

"You two are going to miss lunch," Mrs. Brisbane reminded them.

"Okay." Seth rushed out the door, but Tabitha stayed in her seat. Mrs. Brisbane came toward her.

"Tabitha, I know you've been moved around a lot. Your foster mother told me you've been with five families in four years. But she also told me that she wants you to stay with her forever," the teacher told her.

Tabitha stroked Smiley's fur. "They all say that. It just never works out."

Mrs. Brisbane sat in the chair next to Tabitha so they were eye to eye. "I don't mind having Smiley in class. But I think you'd make more friends if you left him at home. He'd be waiting for you there. You can make new friends without giving up the old ones. Don't you know that little song?"

Now, Mrs. Brisbane has surprised me many times, but I almost fell off my ladder when she started to sing.

Make new friends, but keep the old,
One is silver and the other's gold.

What a beautiful song! And Mrs. Brisbane had a nice voice, too. We were all quiet afterward until Tabitha asked, "What's the good of making friends if you're not going to stay?"

"A person can have many friends in her life. Even if you move on, a friend can be forever. At least in your memory."

Oooh, I felt a little pang somewhere close to my heart. Ms. Mac was the teacher who brought me to Room 26. Although she had to move on without me, she was a forever friend who would always be in my memory. Ms. Mac was pure gold.

"Listen to her! She's right!" I squeaked.

Mrs. Brisbane smiled. "Sounds like Humphrey wants to be your friend, too. How would you like to take him home with you this weekend?"

"I'd have to ask my mom. My foster mom."

"I'll call her right now, while you get some lunch," said the teacher.

I have to admit, Mrs. Brisbane is the BEST-BEST-BEST teacher in the world and also a golden friend. Even if she did let Og into the classroom and made us study frogs.

"To like and dislike the same things, that is indeed true friendship."

Sallust, Roman politician and historian

Test Distress

As Aldo swept the floor later that night, he talked and talked.

"Maria thinks I should take Mrs. Brisbane up on her offer. I don't know, Humph. Can you imagine me as a teacher?"

"YES-YES-YES!" I squeaked.

"I mean, what could I teach those kids? What do I know?"

Aldo spent many an evening talking to me while we ate our dinners. Believe me, he knew a lot! But I'd never seen him act like this before. He muttered while he mopped the floor. He mumbled while he dusted. He argued with himself while he sat down to eat his sandwich.

"Science? Math? History? Which would be best?" he asked.

"Anything except frogs," I squeaked, and to my surprise, Og responded with a "Boing!"

"I bet they've learned a lot from you, Humphrey.

You've probably taught these kids more than I ever could."

I was too modest to answer "Yes."

Aldo dug down in his lunch bag and pulled out a piece of broccoli. "Here's something for you, buddy." He held it up and examined it. "Funny, it looks small to me, but to you, I bet it looks like a great big tree!"

What it looked like was delicious. "Thanks," I squeaked.

Aldo leaned in closer and stared at me. "I guess everything looks different to you, pal." He held up his finger. "I just see a finger, but I'll bet you see every little line and swirl in the skin."

I wasn't quite sure what Aldo was getting at, but I squeaked in support.

Aldo took a long sip of coffee from his thermos. "Of course, no two people see things exactly the same, either. And the more you look, the more . . ."

He suddenly jumped up. "This might be it, Humphrey. I mean, it's interesting, it's different. Like a microscope. Yeah!"

I had no idea what he was talking about, so I munched thoughtfully on the broccoli. (Why some humans don't like it is a mystery to me.)

Aldo wheeled out his cleaning cart. "You always give me the best ideas, Humph! See you later!"

He disappeared but then quickly popped his head back in the doorway.

"You, too, Og. Don't want to leave out my fine froggy friend!"

So, Og was Aldo's friend . . . but still not mine.

I guess the grumpy lump next door didn't know or care, because all I heard from him was splashing.

Tabitha's foster mom said yes. I'd be spending the weekend at her house. But I figured I wouldn't get much attention from Tabitha since all she cared about was Smiley the bear.

There were SO many problems in Room 26. Garth and A.J. were still worried about Marty Bean. Heidi and Gail were still MAD-MAD-MAD. Miranda and Abby were friends now, but would they stay that way without me around to help? I spent so much time thinking about these problems, I forgot the *other* problems in Room 26.

Math problems.

I had been dreaming (the sleeping kind and the day kind) during math for most of the week. When Mrs. Brisbane started reviewing for a big math test coming up, I had no idea what she was talking about!

I wasn't alone. Mrs. Brisbane gave the class a pop quiz and guess what? Half of us failed!

"It's not fair!" Mandy complained, while everybody else moaned and groaned. Our teacher was not pleased.

"All right, class. The quiz won't count toward your grade. But the rest of the school year builds on these concepts. You've got to master these problems," she explained. "I've prepared a study guide for the test next week. I want you to complete this over the weekend."

You should have heard the moans and groans then!

“I’m sorry, class. This is important to me and to you,” Mrs. Brisbane insisted as she handed out the papers. “Put your name on your guide and bring it back—completed—on Monday.”

“I flunked. How about you?” Seth whispered to Tabitha.

“Almost,” she whispered back.

“It’s time for recess,” Mrs. Brisbane said. “Put your study guides in your backpacks now so you won’t forget them.”

Papers rustled as my classmates tucked away their study guides.

The second hand on the big clock circled around. TICK-TICK-TICK. Those study guides made me think up a Plan, but I wasn’t sure I’d have the time to pull it off.

Once the bell rang, the students rushed to get their coats and raced out the door. Mrs. Brisbane gathered up some papers from her desk and hurried out the door. Sometimes she spent recess in the teachers’ lounge. Luckily, this was one of those days.

There was no time to waste, so I flung open my cage door. “Og, don’t you tell a soul what I’m about to do!” I told my neighbor.

It’s not easy to get from my cage to the classroom floor, but I’d mastered a technique. First, I slid down the smooth table leg. It wasn’t difficult, but it was a bit too fast for comfort. The way back was more challenging. I couldn’t slide back up the leg, so I’d grab on to the cord from the blinds and swing myself back up. It was a dangerous undertaking that was always scary. But I had to take the chance because I had important work to do.

Once I hit the ground, I scampered over to Seth's chair. His backpack was on the floor. Happily, he'd left his study guide sticking out of the pocket. I had to use my paws and teeth to pull it out and drag it over to Tabitha's table.

Getting the paper into the pocket of her backpack—which was my goal—was a challenge. Her backpack was hanging from her chair. The pocket I wanted was at least a foot off the ground—awfully high for a small hamster.

By chance, there was a long cord dangling down from the pocket zipper. Holding the paper firmly in my teeth, I grabbed on and tried to pull myself up with all my might.

"BOING!" Og was trying to tell me something, but what?

Just then, the bell rang. It seemed much louder than usual. So that's what he was trying to tell me! He was trying to warn me that I was in serious danger of being caught outside of my cage. I was also in danger of being trampled on by large feet. At least they were large compared to me!

I dropped the study guide and scurried as fast as I could toward the table. With no time to waste, I grabbed the cord and began swinging back and forth, higher and higher.

"BOING-BOING!" croaked Og.

"I know, I know!" I squeaked back. My stomach did

flip-flops as I saw the edge of the table. I took a deep breath and leaped onto the tabletop.

Mrs. Brisbane opened the door and I could hear the thunder of feet as my friends rushed to the cloakroom. I sprinted across the table. Please don't let them see me. PLEASE-PLEASE-PLEASE, I thought as I darted into my cage, pulled the door behind me and collapsed on a pile of wood shavings.

I held my breath, waiting to hear if I'd been caught in the act. I heard Mrs. Brisbane's footsteps approach.

"Why is the cord swinging like that?" she wondered out loud. "That's odd."

Og began splashing like I'd never heard him splash before. "BOING!" he croaked. "BOING!"

"Calm down, Og," said Mrs. Brisbane. "Are you hungry or something?" She told Art to feed him some of his beloved bugs.

Og had made Mrs. Brisbane switch her attention to him, so she'd forget about the cord. For the first time, I was pretty sure that the frog was talking to me—even helping me. Maybe he was friendlier than I'd figured. He'd helped me get back safely, thank goodness, although my mission had failed.

Once my heartbeat had returned to normal, I squeaked a big "Thanks" to Og and looked over at Tabitha's table. Seth's study guide was still lying on the floor near her backpack.

Mrs. Brisbane talked about something called "helping verbs" for the rest of the afternoon. When it was almost time for the bell to ring, Mrs. Brisbane reminded the class about their math study guides.

"Tabitha, I believe yours is on the floor. Put it in your backpack, please."

"Yes!" I squeaked out loud. This was too good to be true! The bell rang. Seth grabbed his backpack and headed to the cloakroom.

Tabitha didn't bother to look at the paper. She just stuffed it into her backpack pocket. Hooray! She also put Smiley into her bag as the other students streamed out of the classroom.

Soon, Tabitha's mom—her foster mom—arrived to pick us up for the weekend.

When I glanced over at Og, he looked a little gloomy, despite that stupid grin plastered on his face. Maybe he wished he could go home with our classmates on the weekends, too. Maybe Og was jealous of me. I had a bad feeling just thinking about that old green-eyed monster again.

Suddenly I felt SAD-SAD-SAD about leaving Og alone for the whole weekend.

"A friend is what the heart needs all the time."

Henry Van Dyke, American clergyman, educator and writer

Study Buddies

Tabitha's mom looked like a regular mom, even though Tabitha said she wasn't her real one. Tabitha called her Carol.

"I've been looking forward to this all day," said Carol, with a smile that showed she meant it. I liked her enthusiasm. "You'll have to show me how to take care of Humphrey. I've never had a hamster before."

"It's a snap!" I squeaked.

"I think Humphrey's trying to tell us something," Carol said. Smart lady!

Once we were home, Carol set my cage on the table and made some hot chocolate. "How was your day?" she asked.

Tabitha shrugged her shoulders. "Just like any other day."

If she only knew!

She opened her backpack and pulled out some papers. "I've got math homework."

Carol examined the paper. "Honey, this isn't yours. It belongs to somebody named Seth Stevenson."

Tabitha grabbed the study guide. "We must have switched." She rummaged around in her backpack and pulled out another study guide. "Hang on. This one's mine." She showed Carol the study guide with her name on it.

"Is this important?" asked Carol.

"Very," said Tabitha.

"VERY-VERY-VERY." I couldn't help squeaking up.

"Seth will need this. We'd better try to call him," Carol said.

It looked as if things were working out according to my Plan, but you can never be sure with humans.

Seth and his mom arrived the next morning.

"Thank you for calling," said Mrs. Stevenson. "Seth was in a panic when he couldn't find his homework."

"It took me a while to get your number. I finally called Mrs. Brisbane," Carol explained.

"I'm sorry we never met before. I didn't even know there was a new girl in the class," Seth's mom said.

Seth and his mother—whose name is June, I found out—took off their coats, and Carol made hot chocolate again.

"I'm so happy to meet somebody from Tabitha's class," said Carol.

"Did Tabitha get invited to Richie's birthday party?" June asked.

Carol shook her head.

"I'll call his mom. She invited everyone in the class, but I'll bet she didn't know about Tabitha, either. I'm sorry no one called to welcome you. We'd love to have you at the parent-teacher meetings."

Carol poured out the steaming chocolate. "I'd like that. I'm kind of new to the mother business."

"Looks like you're off to a good start," said June. The two mothers moved into the living room, while Seth and Tabitha sat by my cage. Smiley the bear lay on the table.

"Hey, Humphrey," Seth greeted me.

I spun on my wheel to show him I was happy to see him.

"If Richie invites you to his party, will you go?" he asked Tabitha.

"I don't know," she said. "Maybe."

Seth rubbed his nose. "Well, if you do, could you leave Smiley at home?"

Tabitha looked surprised. "Why?"

Seth sighed. "Well, *I* know you're not weird, but the other kids think you are because of the bear. If you'd leave him at home, they'd know you're—you know—regular, like them. Then they'd like you."

Tabitha thought it over. "Are you going to be there?"

"Sure. Richie says he's planned a cool surprise!"

Tabitha frowned. "I don't like surprises."

"This will be a good surprise. A great surprise," said Seth.

Tabitha didn't answer right away. "Okay. If you'll be there, I'll come. And I'll leave Smiley at home."

Seth looked relieved. "Great."

They watched me spin on my wheel and talked

about the math test. After a while, Tabitha said, "The basketball game's on. Want to watch it?"

The two of them raced out of the room and I didn't see them again for the rest of the afternoon. June went home, but Seth stayed and she picked him up later. I didn't care because I wasn't worried anymore.

Tabitha left Smiley on the table next to my cage. He seemed to be smiling even more than usual.

It looked as if a nice, shiny, silver friendship had begun.

I felt warm inside all weekend, especially when Seth called Tabitha on Sunday night to ask her some questions about math.

But it was COLD-COLD-COLD on Monday. Shivering, quivering cold.

It was even chillier if you were standing near Heidi and Gail. Even when she wasn't around Heidi, Gail hardly ever giggled anymore.

Then came Tuesday, the day of the big math test. It was probably the quietest day of the year as my classmates were very serious about this test. Kirk groaned a few times during the test. Seth got up three times to sharpen his pencil. Everyone seemed glad when it was over. Especially me.

Aldo was unusually quiet that night, too. Instead of talking to me while he ate, he spent a lot of time writing in a big notebook. Sometimes he'd stop to stare at me, then go back to writing.

It started to snow on Thursday. When the students

got to class, they were all bundled up in heavy hats and scarves and they all had red noses. (A few of those noses were runny, I'm sorry to say.)

After class began, Mrs. Brisbane rubbed her hands together as if they were still cold. "I have finished grading your math tests," she announced. "Every single grade went up. Most of them a lot. I know how hard you all worked and I'm proud of you. Now we can get back to preparing for the Poetry Festival."

When she handed the tests back, there were sighs of relief this time and not one groan.

"Now I have a big surprise for you. Today we're going to have a guest teacher."

"Is that like a substitute?" asked Heidi. Of course, Mrs. Brisbane reminded her to raise her hand.

"No. He's coming in to teach one class. And many of you already know him. It's Aldo Amato."

"You mean my uncle Aldo?" asked Richie.

"Yes, your uncle—Mr. Amato," said Mrs. Brisbane.

And there he was at the door. Aldo had become Mr. Amato. He wore a white shirt, a red vest, dark pants and a plaid tie. He looked almost as spiffy as Principal Morales, and his cleaning cart was nowhere in sight.

"Come on in," Mrs. Brisbane said.

"Thank you, Mrs. Misbane . . . Mrs. Bisbrain . . . Mrs. Brisbane," Aldo stammered. It might have been cold outside, but Aldo was sweating. I was pretty nervous myself.

He turned to the students and said, "Hi, folks. I spend

a lot of time in this classroom when you're not here, so it's nice to see real people sitting in these chairs for once. A good-looking group, I must say."

A few students chuckled, and Aldo relaxed a little.

"I was talking to my pal Humphrey the other night and I started thinking about what the world looks like from his point of view. I mean, here he is, a small animal in a room full of much larger animals. Namely—you!"

When everybody laughed, Aldo looked a lot more relaxed.

"Anyway, Humphrey gave me a funny idea for something we can all try together today."

Who, me? Aw, shucks!

Aldo held up a pencil. "Can anybody tell me what this is?"

"A pencil!" answered Heidi.

"Oops. Hands, please," said Aldo.

Heidi's hand shot up.

"Yes, ma'am," said Aldo.

I was impressed. Mrs. Brisbane never called anybody "ma'am."

"It's a pencil," said Heidi.

"Really? What do you think?" Aldo pointed at Pay-Attention-Art, who was staring up at the ceiling.

"Who, me? What?"

Aldo walked toward Art, holding the pencil up. "I ask you, sir, what does this look like?"

Mrs. Brisbane never called anybody "sir," either.

"A pencil?" answered Art.

Aldo stared at the pencil for a second. "I think you're right. But what does it look like to Humphrey?" Aldo asked.

To tell you the truth, I thought it looked like a pencil, but that clearly wasn't the answer Aldo wanted.

He approached my cage and held the pencil up right in front of me, very close. "What do you think Humphrey sees?"

The class was quiet for a few seconds before hands began going up. Even Heidi remembered to raise her hand.

Aldo picked Kirk this time.

"He probably sees a big strip of yellow," he said.

"I think you're right. What do you think?" Aldo pointed to Sayeh.

"Maybe something grainy. Like a yellow tree trunk," she answered.

"Yeah. If you look closely, you can see the texture." Aldo turned to me. "Right, Humph?"

"Whatever you say, Aldo," I squeaked.

That sent Gail giggling until she caught Heidi's eye. Heidi made a face at her and Gail turned serious.

"So today we're going to look at the world from a Humphrey's-eye point of view. Ready to start?"

My classmates all smiled and nodded. Aldo opened a briefcase—I'd never seen *that* before—and took out an envelope full of tiny squares that were open in the middle, like picture frames.

"These little squares will help us look at things more closely."

Aldo must have spent a lot of time cutting out those one-inch squares. He handed one to each student. Next, he took out all kinds of things from his briefcase and spread them on Mrs. Brisbane's desk. Colored leaves, pieces of lettuce, tomato and broccoli, lemon peel, onion skin, heavy paper, a purple feather, pieces of bread—many interesting and yummy things!

"I want you to draw what you see with your colored pencils or crayons and answer a few questions," said Aldo. "Okay, you can start exploring now."

Soon my friends were wandering around the room, examining things through their square inch. They were so BUSY-BUSY-BUSY, no one seemed to notice that Mr. Morales had slipped into the room. He and Mrs. Brisbane both watched Aldo. They were nodding and smiling.

The kids were smiling, too.

"Ooh, you should see this!" A.J. yelled as he viewed his glove through the square.

I was the only one who noticed that Sayeh went over to Tabitha and asked her if she could borrow Smiley and study his fur.

"He's not here," Tabitha answered. "He's at home."

You could have knocked me over with a purple feather!

While my friends looked at the world from a different point of view, I looked at Og. How did he see the world? His goofy eyes pointed in two separate directions. Perhaps I looked like two hamsters. Or a much bigger hamster than I am. Maybe that's why he leaped at me the first night. It would take more than looking through a little square for me to figure out Og.

After a while, Aldo asked the kids to return to their seats.

"What did you see?" he asked them.

They couldn't wait to share their discoveries. A.J. said his gloves had a million little squares where the lines of yarn crisscrossed. Art's green leaf had a lot of yellow in it and although it seemed smooth, when you saw it up close it was covered with wrinkles. Og's green skin had black dots in it. According to Mandy, my beautiful golden fur was actually brown and white as well as yellow!

"And what did you learn?" asked Aldo.

Gail raised her hand. "That things look different when you look at them more closely."

Aldo smiled broadly. "Good! You learned to *observe*." He wrote the word on the board. "And observation is what scientists do. Sometimes they use microscopes or telescopes to get a closer look. The more you observe, the more you learn. Today, you took a first step toward being a scientist."

Wow, I never knew I was in a classroom full of scientists!

The recess bell rang. As they hurried to get their coats, my classmates thanked Aldo one by one. Finally no one was left except Aldo, Mrs. Brisbane and Principal Morales.

"Excellent job," said Mrs. Brisbane. "I wish you'd come back and get them excited over math."

"Now are you going to send in that application?" asked the principal.

Aldo nodded. "I'm going to do it."

"I'd like to add something to that application. A letter of recommendation," said Mrs. Brisbane.

I thought Aldo would faint. "Would you?"

"I'd be proud to write one, too," said Principal Morales.

"I can't thank you enough," said Aldo.

"Do me one favor," added the principal. "When you graduate and are ready to start teaching, you come to Longfellow School first."

Aldo shook his hand. "I wouldn't go anywhere else," he said.

Whew! That was a relief. I was SAD-SAD-SAD when Ms. Mac left for Brazil. I'd be even sadder if Aldo left, too.

"Tell me your friends and I'll tell you who you are."

Assyrian proverb

Party Hearty

That week, there was plenty of chatter about Richie's upcoming birthday. All that excitement gave me a wiggle in my whiskers and a pounding in my heart. What was this big surprise Richie talked about all the time?

On Friday, Mrs. Brisbane announced that Richie would be taking me home for the weekend.

"Yay! Humphrey's coming to the party, too," A.J. yelled.

I'd never been to a party outside of Room 26 before. Overjoyed, I jumped on my wheel and spun as fast as I could.

"BOING!" Og croaked.

Oops! I realized that Og had not been invited to the party.

"What about Og?" asked Richie. "Can he come, too?"

Mrs. Brisbane shook her head. "I think you have all you can handle. Besides, I'm taking Og home with me. My husband is working on a surprise for him."

"Eeek!" I squeaked. It just slipped out. Mr. Brisbane, whom I hadn't even seen since Christmas, was working on a surprise for the frog? I could feel that green-eyed monster inside me again. I was jealous of a large lump with a ghastly grin and I wasn't proud of myself.

Richie was hopping from one foot to another, like a frog, by the time his mom came to pick us up after school. "We're going to party hearty, Humphrey!" he shouted.

"Try to relax, Richie," Mrs. Rinaldi told him as we got in the car. "If we're going to have this party, you'll have to calm down."

The Rinaldi house was in quite an uproar that night. First of all, there were so many aunts, uncles, grandmas and grandpas there, I wasn't sure which was which.

Everyone was hustling around, moving chairs and putting up decorations in the basement or bustling around the kitchen, cooking. As busy as they were, they all managed to stop and say, "Hi, Humphrey." Or "Isn't he a cutie?"

Uncle Aldo and his wife, Maria, stopped by to help. When Aldo announced he was starting college again, his relatives slapped him on the back and said, "Way to go!" They were as HAPPY-HAPPY-HAPPY about it as I was!

On Saturday morning, there was even more commotion as Richie's family hurried up and down the stairs, preparing for the party. Aldo and Maria came back to help.

Early in the afternoon, Aldo put on a top hat and picked up my cage.

"Okay, Humph. Time for us to party on!"

He carried my cage downstairs to the basement.

What sights I saw there! The ceiling was covered with balloons of every color. Along the walls were brightly colored booths made out of big cardboard boxes. A circle of chairs surrounded a large platform. Happy circus music was playing and I could smell popcorn and lemonade.

Aldo set my cage on a big table and said, "Welcome to Richie Rinaldi's Crazy Carnival! Step right up, one and all!"

Soon my friends from Room 26 made their way down the stairs. Gail and Heidi (not together, of course), Kirk, Garth, Mandy, Sayeh, A.J. and Art, Seth and Tabitha.

As soon as Sayeh saw Tabitha arrive, she hurried over to greet her. "Oh, I'm glad you came!" she said.

Then, down the stairs came Marty. Marty? I blinked hard and looked again. Sure enough, Martin Bean, the guy who's REALLY MEAN, was right there in Richie's basement!

"My mom made me invite him," I heard Richie tell Garth. "He's in my Sunday school class."

There's school on Sunday, too? Gee, you learn something new every day.

The kids all put brightly wrapped presents on a table. Most of them said hello to me. Then Aldo said, "Step right up and play the most amazing games on earth!"

Each of the booths along the wall featured a different activity. Richie's dad had a booth where the kids tossed rings at empty soda bottles. If three rings landed over the bottles, you got a pink ticket.

Cousin Mark's booth featured a game where you threw a small basketball through a hoop. You got a pink ticket for each basket made.

In Grandpa Rinaldi's booth, you had to knock little bowling pins down with a ball. If you knocked them all down, you got a pink ticket.

Closest to me was Maria's booth. She had a flowered scarf on her head and a big glass ball in front of her. "Come, hear Madame Maria tell your fortune," she called to the crowd.

Madame Maria told Mandy that in the future, she would eat "much popcorn." (I think she already had.) Then Maria told Kirk that in the future, he would have a lot of fun. Kirk always does!

There was so much noise in Richie's basement, I was tempted to go into my sleeping house for some peace and quiet. But I didn't want to miss any of the fun.

Then—uh-oh—I noticed someone not having fun. Heidi Hopper was on her way to the basketball booth when Big Mean Bean stood in front of her, blocking her way. She moved to the right to go around him. Marty moved to the right and blocked her.

"What's your hurry?" he asked in a nasty voice.

Heidi moved to the left to go around him. Marty moved to the left and blocked her.

"Say the magic word," said Marty.

"Please," Heidi said in a soft voice.

"Can't hear you!"

"Please!" Heidi spoke much louder now.

Marty sneered. "That's not the magic word. Guess again."

Once more, Heidi tried to go around him and he stopped her. She was almost in tears. This was unsqueakable behavior!

"Let her go!" I yelled. Not that anyone could hear a small hamster over all the hubbub.

Suddenly, Gail appeared out of nowhere. "Stop it, Marty!" she said, and she pushed him out of the way. She grabbed Heidi's hand and pulled her toward the fortune-telling booth. "Come on, Heidi."

Marty stood there with his mouth wide open. I could hardly believe what I'd seen myself. First of all, I thought Gail was mad at Heidi. Second of all, no younger kid had ever dared to push Marty before. Especially not a girl. Gail's a lot stronger than she looks.

"Yoo-hoo, ladies! Fortunes told! Let Madame Maria tell you what your future will bring!"

Heidi and Gail looked at one another.

"Step this way," Maria called to them.

The two girls scurried over to her booth and sat down as Maria stared into the glass ball.

"You will be best friends forever," Maria predicted. Hooray! Heidi and Gail looked happy with their fortunes. As they walked away, I heard Gail say, "I'm sorry I said you were a cheater. I was wrong."

"I'm sorry I called you a crybaby," said Heidi.

They didn't seem to know what else to say, until Mandy raced up and asked if they'd tried the ring toss yet. The three of them hurried off to the booth. Those old, gold friends, Heidi and Gail, were back together at last.

Meanwhile, Marty seemed puzzled by the whole incident. He stood motionless, watching the other partygoers pairing off and having fun together. I guess Aldo was watching, because he marched over to him and said, "If you need something to do, I could use some help giving out prizes."

Marty didn't answer.

"Or would you rather be with your friends? You do have friends, don't you, Marty?"

Marty stood like a statue, staring at Aldo.

"You know, Marty, if you stopped pushing everybody around, people might start liking you. So why don't you come over and do something nice, like handing out prizes?"

Aldo didn't wait for an answer. He put his hand on Marty's shoulder and marched him to the Prize Booth.

Meanwhile, Richie and Seth cheered on Tabitha as she got three baskets in a row. Smiley the bear was nowhere in sight.

After Miranda and Sayeh had each earned a handful of pink tickets, they headed for the Prize Booth. But when they saw Marty there, they stopped in their tracks.

"I'm not going over there if *he's* there," said Miranda. "He'd probably steal my tickets."

A.J. and Art were already at the Prize Booth, trying

to choose from the assortment of little puzzles, paddles with balls attached, and funny cardboard glasses with eyeballs painted on them. Aldo and Marty stood behind the prize table.

"Hurry up and take something," Marty said in a gruff voice. He tried to stuff the glasses in A.J.'s hand. "Move it along."

Aldo nudged Marty. "Give them a chance to decide what they want, Marty," he suggested. "How about a train whistle?" he asked, holding up a big wooden whistle in the shape of a train.

"Maybe," said A.J.

"Paddleball is always good," said Art. "I'll take that."

"Good choice," Marty mumbled.

"I'll take the whistle," A.J. decided. "Thanks."

"You're welcome." It sounded strange to hear Mean Martin Bean say those words.

Kirk rushed to the Prize Booth with a handful of tickets.

"Well, if it isn't Kirk the Jer—" Marty stopped himself before he finished.

"Kirk the Basketball King!" said Aldo. "Pick a prize."

Kirk had enough tickets to get a flower with a bulb attached that could squirt water.

"Good choice," said Marty. His voice sounded different. I guess he wasn't used to saying nice things.

At last, Sayeh and Miranda, who had been watching Marty, finally came forward, clutching their prize tickets.

"Ladies, come get your prizes," said Aldo. "Marty will help you. He likes to help. Right, Marty?"

"Here are some key chains," Marty told the girls as they nervously stepped forward. "Or maybe you'd like this tic-tac-toe game."

Miranda and Sayeh were obviously surprised that Marty was acting like a human being is supposed to act, but they handed over their tickets.

"Thanks, Marty," said Miranda, taking the key chain.

Aldo grinned. So did Marty.

Everybody was having such a good time, I was tempted to open the lock-that-doesn't-lock and join the fun.

While I was thinking it over, Aldo blew a whistle and asked everybody to come to the "center ring" for the big show.

As I watched my classmates rush for their chairs, I realized that I had an excellent hamster's-eye view of the center of the ring. There was no need to plan an escape after all.

Once everyone settled down, Aldo took center stage and waved his top hat dramatically. "Ladiezzzz and gentlemen, get ready to be dazzled by the one, the only, the Amazing Magic Mitch!"

Amazing Magic Mitch turned out to be a tall, skinny man also wearing a top hat. His long blond hair touched his shoulders. He had on an oversized black jacket with a red-and-white striped T-shirt and wore huge red-rimmed glasses.

Aldo applauded and the rest of the audience joined in. Magic Mitch carried a table in one hand and a suitcase in the other. He put the suitcase on the table and pulled out a large black wand.

Now I understood. Amazing Magic Mitch was a magician! I'd heard about magic shows, but I'd never seen one before. My whiskers started to quiver as the act began.

He talked the whole time he performed his act. TALK-TALK-TALK! First, he started out with a card trick. He brought A.J. out of the audience and asked him to pick a card, memorize it and return it to the deck. The magician mixed up the cards and asked A.J. to pick another card. The card A.J. selected this time happened to be the EXACT card he had picked the first time!

"Think it's a trick deck?" asked the magician.

"Yes," A.J. answered.

So Magic Mitch called Tabitha out of the audience. He asked her and A.J. to check the deck of cards to see that everything was normal. It was! Then Tabitha had to pick a card and memorize it. Mitch shuffled the cards all around again. When Tabitha picked another card from the deck—you won't believe it—it was the exact same card she had picked before!

Everybody applauded, except me. This guy seemed a little too crafty for me. I decided to keep a close eye on him.

Magic Mitch asked if he could borrow a coin from somebody. Marty volunteered with a quarter he had in his pocket. Imagine, a grown-up taking a coin from a kid!

Mitch rolled the coin up into a handkerchief and it disappeared completely, right before our eyes. He shook out the handkerchief, but the quarter was gone! Marty gasped. Somebody should have warned Magic Mitch not to make Mean Bean mad.

The magician leaned over and asked, "What's that in your ear?" He reached out to touch Marty's ear and produced a quarter: the same one Marty had given him!

Now, I ask you, how can a coin disappear into thin air and then turn up in somebody's ear? This guy was CHEATING-CHEATING-CHEATING!

Next, Magic Mitch had the nerve to ask if the birthday boy had gotten any paper money for his birthday. Richie came up and gave the magician a brand-new dollar bill. You won't believe what Magic Mitch did with that dollar bill. He folded it all up, took out a pair of scissors and cut it into small pieces! That's the rudest thing I've ever seen. Even Og wouldn't do something like that. Richie's eyes were practically popping out of his head as Magic Mitch took the pieces of the dollar, put them in his fist and waved a magic wand. Nothing happened.

"I forgot to say the magic words!" he exclaimed. "Eeny, meeny, miny, moe, you will see the money grow!" This time, when he opened his hand, the dollar bill was back, all in one piece again.

Thank goodness, or I think Richie would have been pretty angry!

Magic Mitch asked Sayeh and Mandy to help him with a trick where he cut up a rope, did some hocus-pocus and returned it in one piece.

And Art helped him make a glass of water disappear under a handkerchief. I mean a whole glass of water!

I would not invite this man to my house for dinner, I can tell you.

Everybody seemed to like the show, though. They gasped and clapped at everything he did.

Finally, he announced the Big Moment! "Ladies and gentlemen, at this point in the show, I usually make a rabbit appear out of my hat. But today, my rabbit is on strike. So I'm going to borrow your class hamster for this amazing trick."

It took me a few seconds to realize that the class hamster was—gulp—me! Richie came over to my cage and gently picked me up, cupping me in his hands.

"Don't be scared, Humphrey. It's only a trick," he whispered.

I knew that, but I didn't want to be cut up in pieces or disappear into thin air. No wonder the rabbit went on strike.

"Since Humphrey is already here, I can't pull him out of my hat. So instead, I will make him disappear *into* my hat!"

Magic Mitch first held his hat upside down and let anyone who wanted to come up and inspect it. Everybody agreed it appeared to be an ordinary hat.

Mitch took me from Richie and put me in the hat. It

was DARK-DARK-DARK inside and I have to admit, I don't like dark places.

As he dropped me down, he pulled something with his finger and I dropped into a secret compartment at the top of the hat. A false bottom came down over my head. I was trapped in a dark, scary place.

I could hear Magic Mitch's muffled voice saying, "Abracadabra, Humphrey dear. I will make you disappear!"

Whoa! The magician turned the hat all the way over. Now I was laying on my back, feeling a little seasick.

"Humphrey! Where are you?" Magic Mitch called out.

He shook the hat to show that it was empty. Except it wasn't.

"Oooh," I squeaked weakly as I bounced up and down, trapped in this stuffy cave.

I guess nobody heard me, not even Magic Mitch.

I could hear the sounds of kids gasping and shuffling around in their seats.

"Where's Humphrey?" I heard A.J. ask.

"Beats me," said Magic Mitch. He turned the hat around and put it on his head. "Want to see another trick?"

"Bring back Humphrey!" Richie said, in a voice as loud as A.J.'s.

"Humphrey who?" asked the magician. He started to do another trick. I couldn't see what he was doing, since I was completely in the dark.

Well, if Magic Mitch wasn't going to do anything about getting me out of that hat, I was going to do something for myself.

When I squinted my eyes, I could see a pinpoint of light above me. If I could see light, there must be an opening there. I crouched in the little space and reached up with my paws. I pushed. And I scratched. And I pushed some more. I may be small, but I'm strong for a hamster.

I could hear Magic Mitch repeating, "Now you see it, now you don't. Which shell has the pea under it?"

"Bring back Humphrey!" more voices shouted, but Mitch ignored them.

Now I could see a lot more light. The top of the hat was opening from all my pushing. There was a space barely big enough for me to squeeze through. I pushed myself up with all my might and popped right out of the top of the hat! I could see my friends from Room 26, Richie's relatives, and also Marty Bean all staring up at me!

Magic Mitch kept going even though nobody paid attention to him.

There was giggling, pointing, nudging and nodding. The giggling turned to chuckling, chortling, laughing and howling!

"Now you see it . . . now you don't." Mitch sounded confused. "Folks? Are you paying attention?"

I could hear my name being whispered around.

I stood up very tall as everyone stared at me. "Greetings, one and all!" I squeaked as loudly as I could.

This produced shrieks of laughter. I took a bow.

The audience members began to shout my name. They stamped their feet and clapped their hands as they chanted, "Hum-phrey! Hum-phrey! Hum-phrey!"

"Okay." The magician sounded quite annoyed. "I'll bring him back!"

He took his hat off and there I was, eyeball to eyeball with Magic Mitch. He looked very pale. "What are you doing? You've ruined my whole show!"

"It's my show now," I squeaked to him.

"Next time, I'm bringing the rabbit," he said glumly.

Nobody else heard him because all my friends continued to clap, stomp and cheer.

Aldo quickly entered the ring and said, "Let's have a big round of applause for the Amazing Magic Mitch!"

Mitch waved his magic hat—which now had a hole in the top—and hurried away from Richie's basement as fast as he could.

The crowd kept applauding and cheering. I knew they were cheering for me.

"A friend is a present you give yourself."

Robert Louis Stevenson, Scottish novelist and poet

Show Business, Snow Business

My classmates were still talking about the party on Monday. Even Mrs. Brisbane chuckled when Richie told the whole story of my triumphant appearance.

But there was something else to talk about: Og's surprise.

Bert Brisbane had built Og a genuine swimming pool! Instead of a large bowl of water, a whole section of the glass box was water, while the rest of it was built up all around with lush green plants.

It was a terrific surprise and I felt just a tiny pang of green-eyed jealousy. Then I noticed that Og's grin looked more like a real smile this time. I guess we'd both had good weekends after all.

After everyone admired the swimming pool, Mrs. Brisbane got down to business. "The Poetry Festival is less than two weeks away. We've got to finalize our selections, memorize the poems, finish the artwork and make our Valentine's Day mailboxes."

From that moment on, there was a mad flurry of

activity. Some students retreated to the cloakroom to memorize their poems. Others drew pictures for the bulletin board while another group made valentine mailboxes using glue, glitter, paint, crayons, buttons, lace and stickers.

Don't worry. Mrs. Brisbane didn't forget to teach us math, science, geography, social studies and spelling. (Believe me, she'd never do that.) But in between, my classmates worked like crazy on poetry and valentines. Our room mothers, Mrs. Hopper and Mrs. Patel, came in to help for two days.

At night, it was just Og and me in Room 26. I wondered what he had done at the Brisbanes' house over the weekend as I watched him swimming and diving in his new pool. He could make a lot more noise splashing around in it. Each night, I got a little more annoyed, until one night I realized why. Here we were, side by side, but I still felt lonely. We had communicated a little and he'd helped me once, but I still wasn't sure if we were friends.

It was time to find out. I opened the lock-that-doesn't-lock. Gathering up my courage, I walked over to his glass house and said, "Hello, Og."

Abruptly, Og turned toward me. I must admit, my hamster heart skipped a beat. Was he going to leap at me again?

"Look, maybe I haven't been much of a pal to you, Og. Maybe I was even a little jealous. But I'd like to try again."

This time, instead of leaping, he dove into the water

with a gigantic SPLASH! The water splashed up to the top of the box, through the screen, onto my nice, dry fur! And if there's one thing hamsters hate, it's wet fur. My usually fluffy golden coat was drippy, droopy and dull. If Og was looking for attention, he was about to get it.

"Thanks for nothing, Og," I squeaked. "I just want you to know that I have a million friends, so I don't really care if you're my friend or not. So, if you're thinking you should be my pal, just forget it!"

Og just stared at me with that same old smile.

"And remember that time you leaped at me?" I continued. "You didn't even scare me."

Not wanting to press my luck, I scampered back into my cage. I'd finally told him off, but I didn't feel better. Not one bit.

Thursday was the gloomiest day I'd ever seen outside. But inside Room 26, the students were far from gloomy. Heidi and Gail were best friends again. Tabitha was friendly with Seth, Sayeh, Miranda—everybody! The poems were coming along as well.

No one, except me, seemed to notice that it was GRAY-GRAY-GRAY outside. In the afternoon, it began to snow. I hopped on my wheel and watched giant circles of lace float to the ground.

That sounded so good, I wrote it in my notebook. "Giant circles of lace." Those words might turn into a poem someday.

The snow continued falling after school let out. It

was pretty with all those lacy circles tumbling down from the sky. After a while, the lacy circles turned into a thick blanket of white.

It was so quiet, you could have heard a frog burp. Not that Og ever did. He was as silent as the snowflakes.

I knew something was terribly wrong when Aldo didn't show up to clean that night. There were no cars in the parking lot and just one parked car on the street. It looked more like a giant snowball than a car.

I counted the hours until morning would arrive. The snow continued falling until it reached the top of the wheels on the parked car. The carpet of snow was beautiful, but the silence made my fur stand up on end. I missed A.J.'s loud voice, Mandy's complaints and Gail's giggles.

When the bell rang for the start of school on Friday, a funny thing happened: Nobody showed up. Not Mrs. Brisbane, not Garth, not Miranda, nobody. There were no cars in the parking lot, no buses pulling in.

The snow showed no sign of stopping. I was snowed in with Og the Frog!

"A life without a friend is a life without sun."

French proverb

Oh No, More Snow!

It was eerie to hear the bell ring for morning recess, lunch, and afternoon recess when there was no one at school except Og and me.

Staring out at all that snow gave me a chill. The temperature was dropping inside as well. What was it that Aldo had said about turning down the heat at night to save money? I felt even chillier as I realized there was no one around to turn the heat up again.

Luckily, I had my fur coat, my sleeping house and a nice pile of wood shavings I could crawl into to keep warm. I wondered how Og was doing with nothing more than four glass walls, some greenery and an unheated swimming pool.

I dozed for much of the day and nibbled on the stash of food I keep hidden in my sleeping nest. We hamsters are smart about saving up food in case of emergency. But my food dish was empty and my water was getting low.

Between naps, I gazed out the window. There were

still no cars on the street. In fact, I couldn't tell where the street ended and the sidewalk began. Everything was a solid sheet of white.

Og was quiet most of the time and the crickets were silent, too. I was BORED-BORED-BORED all alone in the classroom. I even missed math class! Finally, I hopped on my wheel for some lively exercise. That warmed me up, but it also made me hungry. When I checked my stash of food, the only thing left was a limp tomato stem!

The bell signaling the end of school finally rang. I wondered what my classmates were doing. A.J. was probably watching TV with his family. Garth and Andy would be playing video games. I figured Miranda was cuddling up with Clem. (Didn't his bad breath bother her?) Sayeh was no doubt helping her mom care for her younger brother. And Mrs. Brisbane was probably bustling around her warm, toasty kitchen while Mr. Brisbane built a birdhouse.

They were all warm, all cozy, and all well-fed! They were definitely not worrying about me. Or Og.

I wasn't helping myself by thinking of these things. I decided to work on my poem. What rhymes with "gloom"? Doom!

I slipped my notebook and pencil out of their hiding place behind my mirror and burrowed down in my pile of wood shavings to keep warm.

I promptly fell asleep. It was nighttime when I woke up.

"Hey, Og, do you think Aldo will come tonight?" I asked my neighbor.

Og didn't answer. Aldo didn't come. The snow kept falling.

Around midnight, I heard a funny whirring sound and looked out the window. A huge machine, way bigger than a car, crept down the street like a giant yellow snail with an orange light spinning around on top. It rolled along slowly, then disappeared.

Three hours later, it returned from the opposite direction and disappeared again.

"Did you see that, Og?" I squeaked loudly.

He was definitely ignoring me, and I didn't blame him. I'd said terrible things to him, things he probably understood. Guilt made me feel even colder.

"Og, I didn't mean it when I said I didn't care if you were my friend," I called out from my cage. "I'll forgive you for splashing me if you'll forgive me for saying those things. Okay?"

"Boing?" I think he meant "Okay," but there was something odd about the way Og sounded. Maybe he was hungry, like me. Then I recalled that he didn't need to eat as often as I do. Frogs have all the luck.

The next morning, the snow stopped falling. But the ground was covered and there were still no cars or people to be seen, except for that parked snowball—I mean car.

Even if it hadn't snowed, nobody would have come

to school, because it was Saturday. One week ago today, I was starring in Magic Mitch's show. Now, I was alone (almost), COLD-COLD-COLD, hungry and forgotten.

All my life, some human had brought me food and water and cleaned my cage. I'd been well cared for. I'd never had to fend for myself. But I was a smart and capable hamster. It was time for me to take care of myself like my wild hamster ancestors, the ones who lived in the forests with piles of leaves and pinecones. And all the fruits and nuts they could collect.

Hunger must have clouded my brain because it hadn't occurred to me until that moment that all my hamster food was right on the table. Yummy things like hay, mealworms, grains and vitamin drops. All I had to do was help myself!

I opened the lock-that-doesn't-lock and stumbled out of my cage.

"Og, are you okay?" I called out.

"Boing," he replied weakly. It had been a while since he'd eaten, too. And I remembered Mrs. Brisbane talking about how important it was for frogs to have fresh water.

"I'm going to get some food," I explained. "Maybe I can find some mealworms for you. I don't think I can get in the cricket cabinet." Lucky for the crickets.

"Boing." Og sounded even weaker this time. And he didn't look as green as usual. For a frog, that's not good.

I rushed across the top of the table, slightly faint from hunger. And there they were: a great big bag of Nutri-

Nibbles, a taller bag of Hamster Hay and a giant jar of Mighty Mealworms. Yum! Of course, getting from the table to the top of those containers was a big problem for a small hamster. If I climbed up the bag of Nutri-Nibbles, for example, I would be in serious danger of falling into the bag and getting trapped there. Even though I love Nutri-Nibbles, I didn't want to spend my last minutes on earth being crushed by them.

No, the only sensible approach was brute force. I decided to take a run at the bag and knock it over. The treats would tumble out and I could eat to my heart's content.

I took a deep breath and ran at the bag, yelling, "Charge!"

It didn't quite work according to my plan. I hit the bag with all my might and the bag tipped a little. Unfortunately, then it tipped back the other way and crashed down on top of me!

I wasn't crushed, but I was trapped underneath the bag of treats. There was a little air space around me and I could see a glimmer of light. I could breathe, too. I just couldn't get out.

What I *could* do was yell. "Help! I'm trapped!" I squeaked, although the bag muffled the sound.

I'm not sure why I was yelling. "Help me, please!" probably sounded like "SQUEAK-SQUEAK-SQUEAK!"

I squeaked anyway, and waited.

What was that I heard? "Boing, boing, boing! BOING, BOING, BOING!! *BOING, BOING, BOING!!!*" Followed by a large crash!

I couldn't imagine how Og thought all that noise would help me. Then I heard a new sound: bop-bop-bop. Soon, Og was grinning at me through the slit of light.

That crazy old lump of a frog had managed to hop all the way out of his house, and he'd come to save me! He started leaping at the bag, each time hitting it harder and harder. The bag shifted and the space around me started to open up as I crawled toward him.

Og kept bashing the bag, screaming, "Screee! Screee!" This was a whole new Og and a whole new sound.

The space got bigger and bigger and I crawled along until I could reach out and grab Og. Although I was weak from hunger and all that effort, I managed to grab onto Og's back just as the bag shifted again, flattening out. I was GLAD-GLAD-GLAD I wasn't underneath it anymore.

"Screee!" Og repeated. I pulled myself up on Og's back and he hopped away from the bag.

What a thrill! I was rocking and rolling on his back, like a cowboy riding a bucking bronco! "Yee-haw!" I yelled. "Go, Og! Go, Frog!"

"Screee!" he yelled.

All of a sudden, the lights came on and I heard footsteps.

"Oh, no! Look at that, they're out of their cages." It was Mrs. Brisbane. "They knocked the food over. They must be starving, poor things!"

"Smart little critters," said Principal Morales, chuckling. *"Muy inteligente."*

I hardly recognized those two, bundled up in heavy coats and woolly hats with huge scarves almost covering their faces.

"How on earth did they get out?" Mrs. Brisbane wondered.

"Maybe somebody didn't lock Humphrey's cage tightly," said the principal. "And I guess the frog hopped out of his tank. Look, he pushed the lid off."

So, I have a lock-that-doesn't-lock and Og has a top-that-he-can-pop!

"Never fear, Aldo's here!" another voice yelled out.

A bundled-up Aldo hurried into the room. "Are they okay? The snowplow didn't clean our street until half an hour ago. I was going to walk over here, but the radio said it was too dangerous to go out."

"I know," said Mrs. Brisbane. "Bert and I have been worried sick. If I'd known the storm was coming, I would have taken them home with me. And everybody's called me. All the parents, Angie Loomis—everybody."

Mrs. Brisbane put me back in my cage and gave me a handful of Nutri-Nibbles. Principal Morales put Og back in his cage and fed him some icky crickets (gag!). Aldo went to get us both fresh water.

"It's too cold in here for Og," Mr. Morales said. "He pulled through all right, but I'm going to buy him a heater."

More footsteps clomped across the floor. "We came as soon as we got shoveled out!" said Miranda as she, Amy and Abby arrived.

"The girls have been worried all day," said Amy.

We hadn't been forgotten after all. Heidi's mom, Garth's dad and Sayeh and her dad showed up, too, every one of them worried about Og and me.

I wanted to thank them, but it's not polite to talk with your mouth full.

They all asked to take us home for the rest of the weekend, but Mrs. Brisbane was quite firm. "I'm going to be selfish this time. I'm taking them home with me. My husband would never forgive me if I didn't."

Mr. Morales told everyone to be VERY-VERY-VERY careful on the drive back home. He and Aldo helped Mrs. Brisbane prepare our houses for the trip.

Finally, my tummy felt full. "Og?" I squeaked. "Thank you, my friend! Does this mean you forgive me?"

"Boing!" he answered. Which was an extremely nice thing for a frog to say.

"Real friendship is shown in times of trouble; prosperity is full of friends."

Ralph Waldo Emerson, American poet and essayist

Poetry Festivity

Bert Brisbane was waiting at the door for us. "Hurry on in. It's freezing!" he said.

Mr. Morales helped Mrs. Brisbane carry in our houses and all the bags of food and bedding. "Who knows how long they'll have to stay?" he said.

Mrs. Brisbane went to make a pot of tea, and soon Mr. Brisbane was cleaning Og's tank. Mr. Morales may be the Most Important Person at Longfellow School, but the principal rolled up his sleeves and cleaned out my cage. He didn't even complain about what was in my potty corner. (He did wear gloves and washed his hands afterward.)

"This is a good lesson for all of us," said Mrs. Brisbane as she brought in a tray of steaming cups of tea, a plate of cookies and some yummy pieces of broccoli and lettuce for me. "If you decide to have a pet, you have to take total responsibility."

Mr. Morales munched on a cookie. "I think they took responsibility for themselves. How on earth did such small creatures knock down that big bag?"

"I was wondering about that, too," said Mrs. Brisbane. "I think it was teamwork."

"A frog and a hamster? Never heard of such a thing," said Bert. "I sure wish I'd seen those two." He smiled and shook his head. "I always knew that Humphrey was sharp as a tack, but now we know there's a lot going on in Og's head, too."

"Boing!" Og croaked, and he lunged at the side of his glass box.

Mrs. Brisbane chuckled. "He's feeling better. Looks like he wants to play a game of leapfrog."

Leapfrog is a *game*? Had I been wrong about Og since that very first night? Instead of trying to scare me, he wanted to play?

Like Mr. Brisbane, I wasn't sure what went on in Og's head, but he had some good ideas, like rescuing me. He even had another sound he could make. Nobody knew it but me, and that made me feel kind of special. Like a friend.

The sun came out that afternoon and so did the snowplows. While the yards were still covered with snow, the streets were clear and cars traveled freely again.

Across the street from the Brisbanes, two children built a snowman. Inside the Brisbane house, I was more than happy to run mazes and play hide-and-squeak with Bert for old-time's sake. Og watched from his glass house, but said very little.

By Monday, the roads had improved enough to go back to school. Thank goodness, because the Poetry Festival was coming up on Friday and there was still a lot of work to do.

Some of the students had worked on memorizing their poems or writing them out at home over the long weekend. Most had not.

Garth Tugwell had changed poems three times. On Monday, he changed again. Mrs. Brisbane sent him to the cloakroom to memorize his new selection.

Mrs. Brisbane surprised Kirk by asking for his help. "You've been a lot better lately about knowing when to be funny and when to be quiet," she said. "Now I need your help. We don't want this Poetry Festival to be too serious. We want it to be fun. Would you introduce the poems for us?"

Kirk's whole face lit up. "Sure!"

"Be sure to make it funny," she told him.

By the end of the day on Tuesday, the bulletin board was covered with illustrated poems the students had copied out. Along the edge of the board were cutout pictures of famous poets, from Longfellow to a guy named Shakespeare and a lady named Emily Dickinson.

Late in the day on Wednesday, my classmates finished their valentine mailboxes. What they did with ordinary cardboard boxes was excellent! Some of them were covered with red hearts, glitter and pieces of lace. Others were covered with buttons and lots of paint. Garth's had a big dinosaur on the side. Miranda's mailbox had cutout pictures of her family pasted on: her mom, dad, Abby, Amy, baby Ben and (yes) Clem. Tabitha's mailbox had pictures of basketballs, footballs and soccer balls glued across the outside.

Then—SURPRISE—Mandy presented Og with a green box with pictures of frogs and insects all over it. And A.J. gave me a box covered in golden, furry-looking material. (It wasn't real fur. I checked.)

As nice as that was, I felt SAD-SAD-SAD because no matter how many valentines I received, there was no way I could make valentines for everyone in the class. How could I let them know how much I valued their friendship?

I was still feeling low when Aldo arrived Wednesday night. He was in an unusually good mood.

"It's a beautiful evening, gentlemen. And I have good news to share with you!" he announced as he wheeled in his cart.

"I could use some good news, Aldo!" I squeaked back.

"Boing!" added Og.

Aldo pulled a chair up next to my cage. Instead of pulling out his lunch (or a treat for me), he pulled out a piece of paper.

"Behold my first grade from college. A test in psychology." (I wondered if he was in class with Natalie the babysitter.)

"My grade, as you can plainly see . . ." Aldo held the paper up to my cage. "Is an A! Can you believe it, buddies?"

"Three cheers for Aldo!" I squeaked as I hopped on my wheel for a joyful spin.

"I haven't shown this to Maria yet. I'm saving it for her Valentine's present. Along with some flowers and candy, of course. I think this grade will be her favorite gift." Aldo leaned back and smiled with satisfaction.

Og dove into his pool with a huge splash. I think a little water got on Aldo, but he didn't seem to mind.

"Splash away, Og my friend," Aldo said. "It makes a happy sound."

Og splashed because he was happy? All I'd thought about the splashing was that it was irritating!

Aldo was grinning from ear to ear, almost like a frog. "You see before you a happy man. There's nothing better in the world than to have someone to share good news—and even bad news—with. You see, Maria is my wife, but she's also my best friend."

I stopped spinning because I felt a little dizzy. I'd learned a bit about friendship this year by watching my classmates in Room 26. There were friends who got really mad but made up afterward. There were friends who stuck together through thick and thin. There were friends who reached out to you even when you didn't think you needed a friend.

There were friends who would actually rescue you when you were in trouble. There were new friends, old friends, silver and gold friends.

Later that night, I was SORRY-SORRY-SORRY I'd ever doubted Og was my friend. I hadn't understood that sometimes a frog feels jealous and sometimes he feels splash-happy. But he had come through for me when I needed help. So how do you say thank you to a frog?

I decided to write a poem. Not just a "roses are red, frogs are green" poem, but a poem that said what I really felt.

I pulled out my notebook and started to write.

The next day was spent rehearsing for the Poetry Festival and straightening up the room. (Boy, those kids' tables can get pretty messy.) I didn't pay much attention. I was hunkered down in my sleeping nest, writing my hamster heart out.

Friday was Valentine's Day and everyone was excited. In the morning, the students "mailed" their valentine cards in a big box on Mrs. Brisbane's desk. During recess, the teacher sorted out the cards and delivered them, humming happily as she dropped them in the boxes.

After recess, the students opened their cards. There was a lot of giggling and even some crunching, since Mrs. Brisbane had also dropped candy hearts in all the mailboxes.

Out of the blue, A.J. shouted, "Hey, hold on here!" That got everyone's attention. "I got a card from Martin Bean!"

Seth groaned loudly.

"No, listen. He says he's sorry," A.J. explained.

"I got one, too!" said Garth.

Miranda and Heidi had also gotten "I'm sorry" cards from Marty.

"But he's so mean," Mandy blurted.

"People can change," said Mrs. Brisbane. "I think it must have been quite difficult for Martin to write those cards, and he gave them to me to deliver. Maybe it's time to give him a second chance."

Whew, giving Mean Bean a second chance wouldn't be easy. Yet I recalled that once he got started, he was actually pretty nice when he handed out prizes at the birthday party. Maybe Aldo's talk with him had done some good. No wonder he got that A in psychology.

"I'll give him a second chance!" I exclaimed. Of course, it came out "Squeak-squeak-squeak."

"I haven't forgotten you, Humphrey," said Mrs. Brisbane. She came over to help Og and me with our mailboxes. We received cards from all the students in class. Each one was special, but the one I remember the most was from Miranda.

Though "hamster" doesn't have a rhyme,
I love you, Humphrey, all the time.

She'd figured out how to write a poem with the word "hamster" in it after all!

I had one more card in my mailbox than Og. It was

from Brazil! Yes, Ms. Mac had remembered me with a teeny little card that said, "Humphrey, you will always be a special friend. Love, Ms. Mac."

She'd sent a letter to the whole class, as well, with greetings from her pupils in Brazil.

As wonderful as it was to receive those cards, I kept one eye on the clock all morning, because I had a special mission to accomplish during lunch.

A hamster's work is never done.

The bell finally rang and the students left, which was good. But Mrs. Brisbane stayed behind, which was bad. She busily rearranged all the chairs into a big half circle. She picked scraps of paper off the floor and straightened a few tables. Wasn't this woman going to eat?

At last, she glanced up at the clock, picked up her lunch bag and hurried out of the room. I didn't have much time, so I tore a page out of my notebook, jiggled the lock-that-doesn't-lock, flung open the door and slid down the leg of the table.

Og started boinging in alarm, but I didn't have time to explain.

I raced across the floor as fast as my legs would carry me, straight to Mrs. Brisbane's desk. When I got there, I gasped with surprise. My plan was to climb up her chair and take a giant leap onto the desk. It was dangerous and risky, but sometimes you have to be bold! However, the teacher had ruined everything by moving her chair FAR-FAR-FAR away from her desk, into the circle of other chairs.

Even worse, her desk didn't have legs to climb up. It was a solid block of wood.

My Big Plan was completely spoiled!

The clock ticked away. My only choice was to set the piece of paper on the floor near her desk and scramble back to the table. I grabbed on to the cord from the blinds and began to swing back and forth until I got up to the top of the table. I took the final leap and scurried back to my cage, pulling the cage door shut behind me.

"Boing-boing-boing!" croaked Og.

"You'll understand soon," I told him. "I hope."

After lunch, Mrs. Brisbane returned to the classroom, followed by her other students. The room mothers arrived with punch and cookies. Next, the other parents entered. Everyone was so busy saying hello and admiring the decorations that I lost track of Mrs. Brisbane.

I could hear her, though. "Ladies and gentlemen, if you can take your seats, we're ready for the Poetry Festival to begin." She talked about what we'd been studying and all the hard work we'd put in. Then she turned the celebration over to Kirk Chen.

Kirk was in good form. He introduced each student with a short poem. The rhymes were funny, but they didn't hurt anybody's feelings. For instance, when it was Heidi's turn, Kirk said, "Here's something fun by Heidi Hopper. When it comes to poems, you can't top her!"

He introduced Tabitha by saying, "Tabitha's new, but boy, can she rhyme. We hope she stays a long, long time."

And for A.J.'s poem he said, "A.J.'s poem makes him proud, so don't be surprised if he speaks real loud."

(A.J. did, too.)

I was PROUD-PROUD-PROUD of my classmates as one by one they stood in front of the room and recited their poems. Heidi recited the frog poem she wrote. Instead of her Smiley poem, Tabitha performed a funny poem about a baseball player named Casey. Sayeh recited the dove poem. Pay-Attention-Art lost his place in his poem, but he started over again and did fine. If anybody forgot a word, Mrs. Brisbane whispered it and nobody seemed to notice.

The parents clapped heartily for each and every poem. I did, too!

Then my heart sank as Mrs. Brisbane said, "That concludes this year's Poetry Festival. I hope you'll all stay for refreshments."

My Plan had failed utterly! I glanced over at Og. He was still smiling, but he didn't know what I had planned.

But Mrs. Brisbane kept talking. "I have one more poem I'd like to share. I found this scrap of paper on the floor as you arrived. I think it expresses the feelings the children in this room have for each other. It's very tiny and a little hard to read, but I'll try."

A friend doesn't have to be a work of art,
Just have a heart.

A friend doesn't need to have fur or hair
To care.

A friend doesn't have a thing to do
But like you.

A friend doesn't need to say a word
To be heard.

It's not so hard to be a friend
In the end.

The room was silent until Heidi's mom started the applause and everyone joined in.

"There's a scratchy kind of scribbling at the bottom. I can't make out the name," said Mrs. Brisbane. "Would the pupil who wrote this like to stand up and identify him- or herself?"

I was standing up, all right. And I squeaked at the top of my voice, "I wrote it! I wrote it for Og! It's my valentine to him!"

"Sounds like Humphrey knows who wrote it," Mr. Golden joked, and everybody laughed. Everybody except Og.

"Boing-boing!" he shouted, hopping up and down. At last, I'd gotten through to him. And now I knew exactly what he was saying.

"You're welcome, Og," I replied. "You're welcome, you grinning, green, lumpy, bumpy, hairless, google-eyed, cricket-eating friend. You're entirely welcome."

Later that night, I looked over at Og as he dove into his swimming pool with a giant splash! He looked the same as ever, yet everything was different. What had seemed like a sneery-leer was really a friendly grin. The splashing that once annoyed me made me feel good, because I knew Og was HAPPY-HAPPY-HAPPY. And a lunge that once scared me just meant Og wanted to play a game.

Sometimes humans are hard to understand, especially when they act mean, like Marty Bean, or get crabby, like Abby. But with patience (and a little psychology), you can usually figure them out.

It's the same with frogs. And even hamsters.

I'd made a few mistakes, but I'd managed to keep my old friends in Room 26 and make a new one, too.

Suddenly, my heart went "BOING!" as I thought about my shiny-silver new friend.

My friend Og.

"Of what shall a man be proud, if he is not proud of his friends?"

Robert Louis Stevenson, Scottish novelist and poet

Humphrey's Guide to the Care and Feeding of Friends

1. If you act like a jerk and tease people, you won't have any friends. Guaranteed.
2. If you do the opposite, and are nice to people, you'll have friends. It might take a while, but you'll have friends.
3. If you act like a jerk to your friends and they get mad, but you're REALLY-REALLY-REALLY sorry and let your friends know it, they will probably forgive you.
4. Just don't do it too often. (See Rule 1.)
5. A best friend can be your relative, like a stepsister, or even a wife.
6. People don't always think so, but boys and girls can be friends.
7. Sometimes you may want to be friends with somebody but that person (or frog) doesn't want to be friends back. That seems SAD-SAD-SAD, but it's not, because there are other people out there waiting to be friends with you. You just have to look for them. Keep looking—don't give up!
8. A friend is someone you like to be with and you don't even have to talk. Or squeak.

9. Friendship has its own language. Even if you don't understand the words your friend says, you can understand the meaning.
10. You might not know somebody's your friend until he has a problem and you realize you care.

P.S. Tegucigalpa is the capital of Honduras, a country in Central America. Look it up on the map!